Moving On

Nancy Thurston

aka

Lea Meadow

2011-2013

INDEX

PAGE	TITLE
11	Moving on – a New Beginning
14	Fools – Not All April 1
16	What is a Vacation?
17	Boston Blackie
19	The TLC Corral
21	Remembering Dad
23	Rain
25	Special Events
27	Covered Bridges
29	Why Do I Write?
31	A Pueblo Adventure

PAGE	TITLE
36	The Treasure Hunt
39	For Real
42	Imagine This
44	A Perfect Day
47	We Had a Terrible Disagreement
48	Pretense
51	Excuses
52	Feelings
54	Sunshine
56	Autumn
58	In the Realm of Nancy's Bears
60	The River
63	A Moment of Silence

PAGE	TITLE
65	Reaching In Pulling Out
66	Old Wives' Tales
68	A Wild Winter
69	My Pet Cat Snitched on Me
71	Sunsets Here and There
72	The Raging Fire
73	The Last of the Nuts
76	Who's in my Name?
88	Emily Cady
93	A Job Nobody Wanted
96	Night Sounds
98	Stop that Noise
99	An Object in the Road Ahead

PAGE	TITLE
104	Habits to Live By
108	My Feelings on the Road to Recovery
110	Sled Ride of Winter
111	My Longest Day
114	The Deer Hunt
115	Pictures of My Life
120	My Most Embarrassing Moment
123	Sunshine
125	Time for Confession
127	Fun in the Making
129	The Welcome
133	Santa Wore a Bow Tie
134	How I Controlled my Little Sister

PAGE	TITLE
138	I Saw the Answer in the Firelight
139	Understanding the Look on a Person's Face
141	The Raging River
143	Day is Done
144	Living for the Present
146	Praise for the P
148	A Memorable Family Reunion
154	Love is Warm
156	My Best Habit
158	Oh, No, Another Red Light
161	Once a Day, Every Day
162	I Walked into Quicksand

PAGE	TITLE
165	Growing Up Middaugh
172	Inn Keeping
174	Tell it to the Wind
176	Looking for a Home
178	A Drive in the Country
179	The Birds Flew South
182	Childhood Myths and Other Things
185	When Roads Became Slippery
188	Why do We Procrastinate?
190	A Quiet Dream
191	Living to Learn and Learning to Live
194	A Day in the Field of Learning
197	I Saw a Glimpse of Heaven

PAGE	TITLE
199	The Old Cellar
203	Amazing Facts
204	Strange Noises in the Dark
206	The Family Farm
210	A Tree Climbing Fool
213	A Happy Heart
214	I Entered the Race
216	The Secret Ingredient
217	My Favorite Meal and Where I go to Get It
220	Dad Fell Hard for Mom
221	On a Summer Evening
222	The Winning Number
223	Uphill
225	Let Us Help You
228	Missing You

PAGE	TITLE
232	Looking for a Home
236	More on Love
238	The Light that Twinkled
239	A Mother's Love
242	I Love Books
244	A Call From the Wild
246	The Barn Was Haunted
249	Adventures of My Life
252	About the Author
256	Editor's Note

MOVING ON – A NEW BEGINNING
3/25/11

It seems every twelve years or so, we move, hopefully – on. An over-sized home and too much land were contributors to our exile from Arkansas to Indiana.

However, the really big reason was our love of history and genealogy, the urge to learn more about our heritage.

Although internet exploration has been a great asset, traveling to areas where our ancestors settled, the "eyes on" experience is more rewarding.

The Mormons and their LDS library began our journey over a decade ago.

We attended a seminar where we were introduced to the tool known as the "Internet" and were encouraged to look at the LDS site. Before leaving the seminar we pushed the "search" button, using my maternal grandfather's name. We hurried home to unravel the journeys of those who came before us.

In actuality we have traveled to eastern South Dakota and as far north as Minneapolis, Minnesota, across Wisconsin and into northern Michigan. We have searched many libraries and historical societies there and upstate New York, northern New Jersey, eastern Pennsylvania and western Massachusetts.

Along the way some legendary families tales have been found misleading. Birth records, marriage records and census records have redirected "facts" passed down through the generations.

The most outstanding records regarded the birth date of my mother, which was always celebrated on June 12, six days after her actual birth, but the day she changed from "Baby Girl" to Bessie - one of several names by which she was called. Daddy called her Betty, her parents called her Bess. However, her given name was Elizabeth Margaret.

Our diggings have uncovered other unique changes in the make-up of my heritage. My maternal grandmother was called Addie, short for

Adelaid. Census records indicate her name as Amelia – no reference to Adelaid.

Oh! Census records! Another eye-opening tool known to genealogists. These records are not always correct and neither is family lore. One hopes that birth records, at least, are accurate.

Regarding census records. My father's formal education ceased after his eighth year when farm duties took precedence. In his early twenties he became a census taker in Sioux Valley Township, Jackson County, Minnesota.

His Uncle "Shally" Schlapkohl appears with a number of spelling variations. His name was Charles, but with strong German accent pronunciation it sounded more like Shally. As there is no Charlie or Charles in any Jackson County census records we must assume Shally was how it sounded.

Genealogy research is not limited to family searches, and looking for mine was a side trip.

I own two large oil paintings, both signed by a New York artist, Esperanza Gabay. Esperanza Gabay was born in New York City in 1875. She attended the Art Students League, which still exists in the same building and has graduated a number of well-known artists. Her instructors included several prominent painters of the era, including the landscape painter, Kenyon Cox.

The quest continues, both regarding Ms. Gabay and my genetic profile. Moving from Arkansas to Indiana has shortened travel time by one day, whether going East or West or due North.

Thus a new chapter has begun to grow.

* * * * * * * * *

FOOLS – NOT ALL APRIL 1
Nancy Thurston

My dad loved to play "tricks" on people. One Halloween he decided to be one step ahead of the little people, dressed up in a big white sheet and tucked his 6'3" frame behind the cedar bushes in front of the house.

The first little boy to ring the door bell stopped, looked at the "ghost" and said, "Oh, Ernie - what do you think you are doing in the bushes?" End of that prank!

My first husband had NO sense of humor, as we discovered one Christmas Eve – zilch, nada.

Daddy and yours truly found a nice, long, thin box – one that came from the carpet store – and stuck a broom handle inside, wrapped it all in a paper of the season and put it in the car trunk.

Hubby opened his gifts – not many – the box was brought in – and the recipient began to unwrap the box – shook it – tore into the paper – and when he saw what was inside – he threw that broom handle clear across the room, swearing like the Irishman he was – we ran for cover – and brought in the real box containing a (unloaded) gun. Lesson learned – don't cross a hot headed Irishman - ever!

* * * * * * * * *

WHAT IS A VACATION?
4/13/11

There are good vacations, bad vacations, and those in between. Some are more memorable than others. In three quarters of a century, one should have experienced at least one such trip.

Random House defines a vacation as "a period of suspension of regular work, study or other activity; freedom from something." As it is spring, a season of renewal and hope, what follows is a recounting of a happy nature.

We are adventurers, looking at many facets for spending our idle time. In 2010 we went West – no genealogy, no family to visit, no ties and no time deadlines.

We left home in northeast Arkansas, traveling North to Missouri and quickly turned westward, heading for Kansas. Dorothy Gail and Toto may have been blown away, but we saw nothing of Kansas except heavy rain all the way across that vast state.

What a welcoming sight when we reached

Colorado and about an hour later the rain ceased.

Our first destination was Durango where we boarded a steam driven train to Silverton. This train trip was something we had planned in advance, so our tickets were already in our hands.

From Durango we headed further west to visit the first National Park on our agenda. Next to genealogy and steam trains, our love is the many beautiful National and State Parks which dot this wonderful land.

We strongly suggest that each reader plan a trip somewhere here in the USA. It is not only fun, but educational as well.

Bon Voyage!

* * * * * * * * * * * * * *

BOSTON BLACKIE
5/13/11

We had a very special cat, just one of a litter of many. He was the runt who needed to be bottle fed. His name was Boston Blackie, who always went by the nick name – "B&B".

He loved to travel. If his master rattled the keys, B was right there for the door to open. He'd sit on the dashboard where he had the view of all that went on around him, never missing a trick.

His yard companion was a dog of mixed breed, black, gray and white huge dots, who went by the name of "Woofer." We lived in the country, so more often than not the pets were free to wander.

B's favorite trip was to the bank, where he knew a treat would be waiting for him. At first he received a lollypop, but not having the talent to figure out its intended purpose, the cashiers kept a bag of cat treats on hand. We lived in western Massachusetts. Taxes were really outrageous, so we moved south to northeast Arkansas.

The journey was long – especially for the four-legged children. We had two vehicles – a rented U-Haul with a station wagon in tow. The two legged animals rode in the U-Haul with the cat and dog safely – or so we thought – behind in the wagon. It was raining – cats and dogs when we started.

A State Trooper pulled us over just past the state line in neighboring New York. One very outraged officer gave us the riot act because the station wagon had disengaged itself and was sitting in a ditch with passengers only.

To make the time pass more quickly for the readers – suffice it to say we stopped in the nearest town with a U-Haul agent, got a new hitch to continue the way south with hardly any other misadventures – but that's another story for another time.

* * * * * * * * * * * * * *

THE TLC CORRAL
5/28/11

One morning in early spring I gazed out the kitchen window to behold an unusual sight.

Picture, if you will, a square garden plot, freshly turned turf awaiting the farmer to plant the seeds.

From my window I watched this scene unfold. In the nearest left corner of the garden sat the family cat named Boston Blackie, well deserved for his vibrant black and white fur. In the opposite front corner sat Polly, the black and white dog, quite oblivious to her companion.

This was a small garden plot. On the far end of this square sat two undomesticated beasts, both normally prey for our pets. There was a rabbit and a deer, equally unaware of what sat across the way.

We watched for a very long time as these four creatures continued the standoff at the TLC Corral. The four beasts finished their breakfasts and calmly went their merry ways, never having paid the others one iota of attention!

Such are the wonders of nature.

* * * * * * * * * * * * *

REMEMBERING DAD
6/3/11

There are so many ways to remember my father. He had no sons, just three daughters, each as different as night and day.

The oldest daughter was named Virginia Elizabeth, but was always called Jimmy. She was three months shy of her eleventh birthday when I made my appearance, a real tow-head blonde in a family of dark-haired individuals.

When both our parents were old enough to know better, Margaret Ann, always called Peggy, joined the family, dark hair and long finger nails. That's when daddy began coaching Little League, surrounded by his adopted boys!

We girls always called him Daddy, even when we were adults with children of our own. He loved to play cards, poker his favorite. He had cronies who were all avid poker players. <u>Nothing</u> interfered with a poker session! We had a three story colonial in which the basement was divided into two sections, one for storage and laundry, the other a large recreation room. A poker night always included a case of cold beer.

One such evening he carried a case of cold beer down the stairs. About half way down, he lost his footing and proceeded downward on his hind quarters. He picked himself and the beer up, and continued down the steps.

He must have spent a very uncomfortable night playing poker and drinking beer, for the next several days he lay flat on his back. But he was tough – no doctors for him!

Ernie – his given name was Ernest – loved to play practical jokes. Sometimes they backfired. Once he hid himself behind the bushes at the front door. His plan was to emerge, dressed in his white sheet, when the Halloween tricksters came knocking. The boys weren't fooled at all, to Daddy's dismay.

Another time he and some of his brothers locked the youngest brother in the outhouse down at the lake. Laughing they continued to shake that two-holer with Ed inside begging for mercy.

I nearly blew Daddy's patience on several

occasions. When I was eleven or twelve I decided to help by backing the car out of the garage. I almost succeeded in taking the entire garage wall with me. Another time when I was having a driving lesson, a cow had the audacity to stroll into the middle of the country lane just as I was approaching. In dismay I pleaded with Daddy – "What do I do now?"

Life with Daddy, always fun – well, usually.

* * * * * * * * *

RAIN
6/17/11

Rain is fickle. We lived in a rather typical two story farm house which sat on the corner of two well-kept rural roads.

George and I were in the back end of the house in the harvest kitchen. Daughter Cindy had just come down the front stairs and looked out the front door.

Easily excited, she told us to come quick — the road was literally being washed down the road, taking some of our front yard with the gushing water! Needless to say, it also left some of the gravel road in our front yard! This Massachusetts phenomenon is just one of several such occurrences.

During our years in Arkansas we have experienced other weather happenings. We lived high on a hill. The village was down the road — way down. The rain decided to do away with the town and came close to achieving its goal. The only building on the river side of the highway that dissected the little town was the Post Office. Ten years after the flood, water marks are still visible inside the Post Office.

We haven't lived in Indiana long enough to have been here during the "Big Flood" but long enough to see how the local park swims in high water.

As a child I saw the mighty Sioux River in Sioux Falls, South Dakota and also in Sioux City, Iowa merrily exceed its banks.

I remember us donning our swim suits and wading down the water filled street in front of our house, which, thankfully, sat on a small hill.

We may feel that Nature is cruel at times. However, She is just reminding the human race that we are not as supreme as we think!

* * * * * * *

SPECIAL EVENTS
6/24/11

As a lover of music, living in western Massachusetts, it was always with the greatest anticipation that we looked forward to the Boston Philharmonic Orchestra to open the doors of their summer home at Tanglewood, near Stockbridge.

I would pack a substantial picnic basket, a couple of blankets to spread on the lawn and pile the three young children into the car.

Our favorite conductors were Seji Osawa and Leonard Bernstein. Osawa was small and quick, a delight to watch. Leonard was tall and forebiding.

One Saturday I decided we should watch a rehearsal, which was held inside the "shed". Bernstein was conducting.

My eight year old daughter espied something that caught her attention. In an excited somewhat loud voice she got my attention – and that of the great maestro himself. Mr. B. stopped the orchestra and turned to warn that such outbursts were not to be tolerated.

Our favorite performances were the Fourth of July. Sousa was usually the highlight of the musical performance. The concert always ended with the 1812 Overture and fireworks displays that were literally out of this world, reaching loud and high above the foothills of the mountains of western Massachusetts.

We learned to rush to our car and leave the parking area before the display, toward its climax. We would stop on top of the highest hill and watch the display over the lake. A truly great ending to a spectacular day.

* * * * * * *

COVERED BRIDGES
7/6/11

While waiting for our new home in Indiana to be constructed, we decided a hobby would be a good way to pass the long days. We were cooped up in an apartment; walls were closing in on us.

So we took to the road. First we explored McCormick's Creek State Park. Knowing that we would likely visit Indiana parks, we invested in a life time park pass, and continued to spend several hours touring the park.

We moved along Hwy. 231 north of Spencer to Cataract, where we found the Cataract Falls Park. There are two falls in the park, Upper Falls and Little Sister. The park is also home to Cataract Covered Bridge.

In 1838 State law gave County Commissioners power to build bridges for "public convenience", as flooding in the Eel River was a transportation nightmare.

On a visit to the Owen County Public Library a book on bridges of the Midwest uncovered a pastime that kept us on the go throughout Indiana.

Heading north on 231, we began "bridging" in earnest. In Putnam County on 231 we found the Dunbar Bridge which was built in 1880 by J.J. Daniels over Big Walnut Creek. Today it is a bridge going nowhere, in other words, it has been bypassed. A plaque at the Dunbar Bridge states, "Early bridges were covered to prevent damage from weather." It was a two-span bridge, allowing vehicles to travel in two directions.

Further north off 231 stands the Okalla Bridge built in 1898. Putnam County has a number of covered bridges.

Author's Note: The previous writing is to be incorporated into a book devoted to the covered bridges in Indiana. Our interest waxed while perusing a book on covered bridges of the Midwest. Only a few Indiana bridges appear in that book.

* * * * * * *

WHY DO I WRITE?
Lea Meadow 8/8/11

The material I wrote on January 9, 2004 will basically tell the tale of why I write. I had gone through the long and tedious process of obtaining a divorce in 1979, for several reasons. The most prominent being the fact that I no longer loved the man I had married. He was a heavy drinker who had turned into what is classified in AA as chronic/incurable. The catalyst came from my counselor who was helping me break the ties. She said "write, don't stop, forget the grammar."

A journal was started in which I wrote diligently. Feelings were the prominent entry. I was told that my writing is stilted. As years go by my journal has become more of a travel log and events of the day just gone.

How does one overcome the high school journalism instilled by the "who, what, where and when" and concentrate on the HOW it has effected your day? In 2004 I decided I would achieve this by being more open with myself, finding expression, a willingness to let go. I stated I would really love to write, BUT I am so afraid. Ah, yes. It is difficult to actually WRITE IT DOWN, those intimate thoughts you hide so well.

Now it is 2011 and I am no longer afraid to say what is truly in my heart. No, I don't go up to someone to harass them but I will tell a young mother that her child is back in the candy department feasting on an unpaid delectable.

From that journal: "I love watching the sun rise – the colors are so subtle – sometimes it is pastel, sometimes bright orange and red. The sunrise is prettiest reflecting off the trees and clouds in the west; same is true with sunsets; the eastern sky lights up from reflections."

* * * * * * *

A PUEBLO ADVENTURE
Lea Meadow

Have you ever dreamt of being a Native American of the West? My name in your tongue is *Laughing Water* and I am eight years old. I have two older brothers who are braves, *He Who Frowns* and *Angry Son*. My father is *Chief Big Hawk*, the shaman of our tribe, and my mother is called *Birdsong*, who is the medicine woman.

Come with me as we climb the canyon in the Pueblo fashion for an adventure of a lifetime.

The warm Arizona sun beats down toward the base of the magnificent canyon. Father has gone hunting the Bison who roam the mesa above us. Mother needs water to make the delicious cornmeal bread for our midday meal, and I have been delegated to fetch this staff of life.

I grab the pottery water vessel and begin the climb down to the stream at the base of the canyon, probably 750 feet below our cliff house. My brothers are all older than me, and have joined the warriors on the hunt. Girls help their mothers with the chores that keep our families safe and happy. Fetching water for an eight-year-old girl should be an easy task, don't you think?

The descent to the stream we travel without incident, unless you consider a stop to chat with two squirrels and a mountain goat unusual. After splashing in the cool waters, I fill the water bowl and start the climb toward home. The trick lies in not spilling any of the precious water on the return trip. But I am agile and my feet know the way to climb from one jutting stone to the next. Many hands have traveled this path before me, and the smooth surface of the rocks makes climbing easy. With the water safely secured to my backpack, I start for home.

The canyon echoes with the sounds of Nature all around me. In the distance the mournful sound of the coyotes still sends a chill down my spine. A mountain goat causes several rocks to cascade down the canyon wall not far from where I climb. A lone wolf howls from the other end of the canyon and the swallows are busy in their flight looking for bugs and other flying insects. If you are very quiet and imaginative, you can hear *Kokopelli* playing his flute. *Kokopelli* has become an icon of fertility in later centuries and probably originated with the *Hopi*, not the *Pueblo*. There are *Kokopelli* kachina everywhere. A kachina is a doll, usually made of cornhusks and cornmeal. I could write another story just about this doll, but then I would be telling stories that have evolved since my time. I am not alone in my journey.

When climbing the canyon it is very helpful that you keep an eye open for snakes for some of them can be quite harmful, shooting their unsuspecting prey with a venom that can kill a person.

So I am ever mindful of that misadventure! The canyon is home to the rattlesnake and others. So far we have not seen a snake; we appear to be alone in our journey.

Arriving home without incident, I find Mother in the small storage room. Our home consists of a number of sleeping rooms, the large center room with the fire pits where Mother cooks our meals and several storage rooms. There are no exterior walls, as our dwellings are built into the canyon crevices and protected from weather, hot and cold. Although the days may become quite warm the nights are cool. In winter the cold winds that are trapped in the canyon bring snow to the higher elevations.

My day has just begun. *Birdsong* next sends me to the mesa to check on our garden, which primarily consists of maize, which is ground for the meal that makes the bread, squash and peppers, which add a tangy taste to our food. My father, *Chief Big Hawk*, is concerned that our dried meat supply, which hangs in the larger storage room, is becoming low and with the approach of the shorter winter days, must be replenished. In addition to the Bison, he hunts for rabbit and squirrel. Father is a hunter/gatherer. My brothers are both very good fishermen, and bring home many river trout and other fresh water fish, which are also hung to dry, that supplement our diet.

Although we Pueblo Nation call these dwellings our home, we did not construct most of them.

The Aztec were here before us, and many of the structures, which are built into the canyon walls, were made by them. Our village is quite large with five dozen families sprawled along the cliffs. We have several *kivas* where the clan meets to discuss important issues. A kiva is a large meeting place. A plaza surrounds each of the *kivas*, where we children gather to play ball, pick-up-sticks and the ever-popular hoop. It becomes quite noisy in the village when the children all gather.

After I have picked the garden of ready product, Mother calls me for our lunch. The afternoon is spent with play. Father and my brothers will not be home for several days, when they will bring the fresh meat.

Evening descends quickly in the canyon and we prepare for a long sleep. And so goes my day in our Pueblo village. Thank you for sharing this day with me. We may do it again in some future time, when white and red skins find peace and harmony.

* * * * * * *

THE TREASURE HUNT
Lea Meadow 8/19/11

My name is Charlie Chang, a recent immigrant to America. With my wife, LiLang, we operate a dry cleaning establishment near the bay in San Francisco.

Three weeks ago, a stranger entered our shop and left his jacket to be cleaned. Because LiLang is a meticulous woman, we always check the pockets on items brought into our shop.

"Oooh" was all LiLing could say, so I grabbed the piece of paper from her hand and looked carefully at what appeared to be a document of some kind. A closer look showed it to be some kind of a map, probably from older times.

The more I studied it, the more obvious it became that it was a *treasure map*! My curiosity got the better of me, so I decided not to return it to the owner, who shall remain anonymous for my protection! Which is a very lucky thing, as this story will soon disclose.

LiLing was very upset with me for keeping the map. She said it is an immoral thing for me to do, but I finally persuaded her to keep still. The map showed that the treasure was buried near our shop in the bay! The map indicated a large, oblong crag near the water, which I could see from my front window! The map showed that buried near the crag there is an old black travel trunk, left by sailors at the time of the big gold rush!

I stopped at the hardware store down the street to purchase a good digging shovel, and ran to the crag. It was warm, and it didn't take long for me to work up a sweat, as I dig and dig some more! In a hole about fifteen feet (or so it seems) my shovel met resistance. I scraped at the object and soon saw a black trunk! Just as written on the map!

I am so excited! But it is hard to bring the trunk to the surface, so I yell for LiLang to come help me. She is still very upset that I am doing this "immoral" thing, as she calls it! But she comes, if only to shut me up. We get the trunk out of the hole, and carry it back to the shop. It takes me five hours of constant struggling to open the trunk. I am dismayed to find nothing but a bunch of very old clothing inside. Now I am frantic and am very determined to continue the search. Looking through layers of Chinese clothing I discover a packet of old letters, written in Chinese, from a dialect I have seen in the old country in my father's home. How fortunate for me, as I can translate them!

What a treasure this has become! These are letters from an ancestor of mine that were never mailed! This man came to America to work in the gold mines! For whatever reason, he chose to bury the trunk, rather than mail the letters! How strange is life!!

* * * * * * *

FOR REAL
Lea Meadow 8/19/11

My sister and I had just experienced a delightful day on St. Simon's Island fifty miles south of Savannah, Georgia. The sun cast a lovely shadow over the lighthouse. The tide was coming in and the fishermen all seemed happy to be spending their day on the dock. We bought several items at the gift shop and headed to a highly recommended restaurant for a feast of crab cakes and peach cobbler.

It was late afternoon, time to head north to Savannah. About ten miles from our destination, storm clouds covered the sky. The wind blew with an intensity not needed while on the road or even just being out-of-doors. Then the skies let loose with a downpour of great magnitude and the temperature fell at least fifteen degrees, all within a few quick moments of time.

Peg has a 2005 Chrysler *Crossfire*. For those not privy to the world of sports cars, this is definitely one of them. It is LOW to the ground.

When the roads begin to flood, you know just how "low" low is, and that the road was definitely flooding.

The windshield wipers were on maximum speed. The AC was working, but the windshield was clouding up even faster than the rain was falling. The blowers didn't seem to know their function and we were enveloped in a fog, both inside and outside of the car. There was only one thing to do. Pull over on the shoulder and pray.

Although there was a box of Kleenex in the car, the tissues couldn't absorb all the moisture building on the inside. There was a paper towel that Peg had used to clean the outside of the windshield when we had stopped to fuel up. Somehow, using this technique caused a terrible film to develop on the inside of the windshield.

As soon as the rain let up, Peg got out and tried cleaning off the outside of the windows in an effort for us to continue to Savannah. We hobbled to a service station along the highway that was preparing to close. Two young men were not much help. They suggested that we just sit there until the weather improved.

It did, but the windows never caught up with the letup. We made it to the hotel, parked the car and set off on foot for a late evening cappuccino and delectable dessert. We would deal with the past crisis in the morning. We'd had enough excitement for one day.

This could end here, but it won't. The next morning we slupped to a Chrysler dealership for the diagnostic test which should indicate the problem. It would take a half hour to run the test, so we opted to walk to the nearest drugstore to buy film and an ace bandage for a bad knee. That walk was a good four mile hike round trip. The blowers? Nothing wrong with the mechanics, just a quirk of Nature working too fast for technology to keep pace.

* * * * * * *

IMAGINE THIS
Lea Meadow
(another story for another time) 8/26/11

Never in my dreams did I anticipate that one day I would need to write an essay or fiction which included any of the following, let alone all of them combined: a) a gnarly paint brush with a yellow handle, b) Kleenex, c) a Sharpie pen, and or d) Hard as Nails. Imagination, get thee to work!

A painter I never believed I could be, unless it was refinishing a piece of furniture. Then I joined a writers' group with all kinds of crazy suggestions for an assignment. This is what evolved.

Allergies are an infliction some of us must endure. Labor of any intensity can include allergic reactions, imagined or otherwise. While attempting to refinish that one hundred plus year old desk, I reached into my purse to extract my eyeglasses. They must have ended up down at the bottom of that rather large purse, so I dumped out the contents on the dining room table.

What a surprise to find that missing yellow

handled paint brush, which I would definitely need to do this job. A rather well used Kleenex went promptly into the trash can, no intrinsic value there. My Sharpie pen had seen better days and was determined to be destined for the same location as the Kleenex.

I dipped the brush into the can of paint. When I went to apply the paint, it met a considerable amount of resistance. The brush had lost its ability to bend, as it had not been properly cleaned and stored after the previous use, which could have been a lifetime away.

Sneezing, I quickly ran for a new Kleenex from the bathroom. The phone rang. A long lost friend from another era and another location was on the line (how's that for a phrase . . . how does a body hang, droop or stand on a line?) Another possible writing assignment, you query? Really!

To end this saga, safely say that the task at hand fell by the wayside. Both the brush and the Kleenex were hard as nails and I had never relished doing that job in the first place. Allergies and lethargy ruled the day. Coffee, here I come.

* * * * * * *

A PERFECT DAY
Lea Meadow 9/15/11

What is a perfect day? We have probably all experienced such an occasion. Mine was June 27, 1981. Two best friends joined hands in matrimony.

The sky was a beautiful blue, not a cloud in sight. I was enthralled by the magnitude of what was to transpire later in the day. It would be perfect, no matter the obstacles one might encounter. We were to become one family shortly after one p.m.

The glitch happened shortly after breakfast. My dear friend and neighbor baked our cake. She was incapacitated and asked if we could please pick up the two wedding cakes. One was traditional with a small figure of a bride and groom planted securely in the middle. The other one was definitely not traditional, but a favorite of the bride and groom . . . a carrot cake with luscious sour cream icing. We have made many of these over the last thirty years, but none compares with the anticipation of that first taste.

Between the two of us, we were parents of eight children from previous marriages. The oldest was my daughter, my son, John, was in the middle of the mess and Michael was the youngest of my children.

George has two sons and three daughters. At the time, all eight were between twelve and nineteen, all served as maids of honor and groom's attendants. His best man was our best friend, the man who had the privilege of introducing us a short year before.

My children were the only members of my family who came to western Massachusetts to participate in the day. Both George's parents and younger sister were there.

My faithful girl friend decided that the ideal spot for this happy occasion was high on a hill on the farm operated by her father.

We left the crowd behind and climbed into the Pontiac Firebird for a trip to upstate New York in the Adirondacks, the home of good friends who were going away for the week and graciously gave us the run of the place. They had an ulterior motive as they needed someone to babysit the Irish setter. Other than a bad habit of drooling with every other intake of air, he was a beautiful creature, and gave us a diversion.

I mentioned that it was a beautiful day. Trust me, George more than likely figured it was the only comment I could conjure upon. And by the time we arrived at our destination, which I repeatedly vowed was just around the next curve, no the next, etc., I'm sure he doubted my ability to give directions. However, I am the official map navigator on our many trips since that beautiful, perfect day.

May the next thirty years be as perfect.

* * * * * * *

WE HAD A TERRIBLE DISAGREEMENT
9/23/11

Sisters frequently don't see eye to eye, and we were no exception. But rarely were we known to carry it as far as a grudge, except that time when our perceptions were not in agreement.

I must confess that for a great number of years I was unaware that a problem existed. After twenty years of not meeting each other face to face, I was in for a big surprise. An icy reception greeted me when at last we were in the same room. I just figured my sister was having one of her snits, and it would dissipate shortly.

I could not take this chilly atmosphere and bravely asked if there was a problem. Oh, yeah, a problem that had been smoldering for eons. It seems that my sister felt I had let her down by not coming home when our father passed away. That was a surprise.

How well I remembered the journey from western Massachusetts that March morning. It was necessary to travel some 90 miles to catch a plane THAT WOULD TRAVEL EAST to Boston before flying over the Great Lakes, taking a layover in Chicago and then on another plane, continuing to Sioux Falls, South Dakota.

I do NOT remember if I arrived much ahead of the funeral, but I know I was there. I viewed him in an open casket, said my goodbyes and watched the ceremony that ensued. The rest is a blank.

I sometimes believe in my heart of hearts that she still carries a certain degree of resentment and disbelief. However, we have shared many happy moments together or on the telephone since. For all outward appearances, we have moved on.

* * * * * * *

PRETENSE
Lea Meadow 10/7/11

(Oh, well, I knew we were supposed to write about something that started with a "P". I'm not sure how I got from preservation to pretense!)

According to my "Reader's Digest Oxford Complete Wordfinder": 1) pretending, make believe; 2a) a pretext or excuse; b) a false show of intentions or motives (and continues). I will use the definition of 2b above.

It was necessary for me to find an excuse in order to enter the saloon for a quick beer after school. I was a freshman in college and rather gullible, someone who loved the challenge of a precocious act.

Mother had made me a very practical reversible coat. It was a peach color corduroy on the outside, lined in a plaid of blue and peach, with HUGE pockets on the inside. My older sorority sisters enjoyed having their freshman pledge accompany them on weekend excursions to the local pub in the neighboring town.

My coat was an excellent hiding place for a bottle of hard liquor (which was a no-no in the town where the University was located.)

Of course, I was only eighteen, under age by about three years, but daring. I basked in the glory of being included in these weekly soirees. I could handle just so much beer, however. The next morning would find me with a tremendous headache with one desire: to be left alone.

Pledges spent the first year in the dorm, not in the sorority house. I was so popular that by the second semester I had a room in the house, well established as the #1 carrier of all provisions.

Meanwhile, back at the dorm. All decorating of rooms was the responsibility of the occupant. My mother was a very good seamstress and made a pair of beautiful brown and pink plaid drapes for the window. Some fifty years later, those drapes are still in my possession.

So, several weeks after school had started, my parents came to town with my drapes. I was still under the influence of the imbibed beverages consumed the previous evening when they arrived. Mother took one look at her delightful daughter and promptly marched me to the coffee house, where I was literally forced to down multiple cups of java.

You query (and quite assuredly deserving)

"so what is the pretense here?" MOTHER saw through my feeble attempt at "cover-up" that I was decidedly hung over, and under the guise of pretense, she removed me from the very innocent eyes of Father, leaving him unattended to hang those drapes.

Daddy probably recognized the situation for what it was . . . a pretense of using a cup of coffee as an excuse to NOT be underfoot. I never asked, he never said.

* * * * * * *

EXCUSES
Lea Meadow 10/14/11

I'm not a poet – that's my excuse –
I have no excuse.

Teachers were given every known excuse
Why homework was lost.
That's my excuse.
What is my excuse,

Not my pen on the loose,
I have no dog – nor neither a moose.

I have no use
For lame alibis or abuse
Nor someone who claims
Being my muse.

What is the cause of this excuse?
Maybe I just have no excuse.

* * * * * * *

FEELINGS
Lea Meadows 10/20/11

    What a perfect day for that topic. My feelings today are all physical, which is probably not the type of feelings the subject indicated.

    My feet and ankles have been bothering me for about two weeks. I finally broke down and saw a doctor. The conversation was convoluted, thus as I write a question lurks in my brain. Did we ever actually discuss the word "fibromyalgia" or just "tendonitis"?

The doctor ordered 3 x-rays to be taken, which was promptly done. I sit here waiting to hear the results, but the phone is silent. Meanwhile, the achy, tingly sensation persists in both ankles, reminding me that discomfort is not one of the feelings I like.

Ah, what feelings should I like? A good meal in good company; bright sunshine beaming through the window; soft, cuddly blankets on the bed, to name a few would be lovely. A certain contentment while sitting around a blazing fire; laughter with friends and family are good feelings. A compliment given at a moment when self-esteem needs to be bolstered or appreciation garnered for something given to a stranger on the street. The little things can mean so much.

Other than physical pain, what are some of the feelings that I probably wouldn't want to harbor? Some words that come to mind are resentment, jealousy, anger, impatience, and rudeness. The lists for good and bad feelings are endless. We all experience feelings of the pain, whether it be an ache in the body or an ache in the heart, such as the loss of someone or something dear to us.

Certain expressions come to mind. "Do you feel the pain?" "He's such a pain in the neck." "The pain Mary Jane." "Does it cause you pain?" "The pain I went through to collect everything to take with me." The list continues with YOUR pain.

* * * * * * *

SUNSHINE
Lea Meadow 10/28/11

As I sit here pondering the concept of putting into words a connotation of perception of the word "sunshine" the sky is overcast with patches of sunshine in the atmosphere. However, I would hesitate to call it a *sunny* day.

"Sunshine on my window makes me happy," as the lyrics to an old favorite tune go through my mind. "To bask in the sun" is another phrase. To write about sunshine in any poetic text would be an affront to Robert Frost or Keats. I will now give some time to describe sunshine and me.

I find it easier to work or play when the sun is shining. On a dull day I am more prone to reading what someone else has written. Edgar Allen Poe would find some gloomy topic to put in verse on such a dreary day. Poetry is not my forte. IF I were to write a poem it would be in the hours between dark and dawn when the world is asleep. My problem being it is dark, a light would need to illuminate the scene and I would then be in another world where poetry escapes me.

I have been known to take pen and paper in hand while reclining in bed in the dark. Funny stuff to look at with the lights burning, disjointed crooked lines all swarming together. In the morning when I peruse the material, I would likely chuckle and vanity would make me save it, but hidden away where other eyes might never see it. I have done that. I would never just throw it away or alter it in any way.

Sunshine conjures joy, happiness, merriment. How can one be gloomy and depressed on a bright sunny day?

* * * * * * *

AUTUMN
Lea Meadow 10/28/11

Autumn leaves are falling all around us here on top of Windy Acres. But our rake will remain standing at ease in the garage for now. Our 3.29 acres are bare of trees, with the exception of the lone Russian Olive tree at the back of the house and a very small tulip poplar at the end of the cul-de-sac. Where, if and when we grace this spot called home with any addition of trees or shrubs will wait until Spring when we have endured our first Indiana winter.

Windy Acres is the nomenclature that I unceremoniously dubbed this lovely spot. It is hopefully the final residence in our journey from place to place over the span of our lifetime.

Generally I have a difficult time deciding which is my most favorite season – Spring or Fall. Spring brings memories of the first tulip to show its head through the snow and ice, a time for rejoicing and giving thanks to the end of drab winter. Fall reminds us that the lush greenery of Summer is fading, a time to reap the harvest and put the earth to rest.

Autumn generated nostalgia as we recollect the lazy hot days just past. It brings the urge to get in the necessary supplies to withstand isolation as the snow falls and buries the egress and exit into the world of other living humans.

We enjoy the solitude. Give us food and a warm atmosphere and we will be content. Good books and games to play in front of the fireplace where the artificial logs blaze embracing us with their warmth. We have gathered together provisions to keep our tummies full and hot cocoa and tea to sip as we watch the wonders of Nature all around us.

* * * * * * *

IN THE REALM OF NANCY'S BEARS
Lea Meadow

My name is Scotty. As the Elder Bear of Nancy's menagerie, it has befallen me to recant the tales of her bears. With me is Cinnamon, her newest acquisition. Let me begin.

Nancy's neighbor and good friend in Egremont, Massachusetts stitched and stuffed me as a housewarming gift. I was joined by two Stieff bears, one dark the other light in color. Alas, it is with great sorrow that these two fine specimens have not been located from their winter abode since moving to Indiana from Arkansas.

Let me see if I can remember all these missing little ones. There are fifty State Bears, small in stature, but each a different color and bearing a United States quarter which depicts the state they represent.

Two of my kin you recently met. They are rather intelligent, or so they like to tell us, as they 'speak'. Well, la-te-dah! The rest of us just laze around, looking cuddly.

I was not Nancy's first bear, however. She received a gift from a doting aunt and uncle. "Teddy" was probably loved to death. If I recall, the teddy bear is said to be so named after Theodore (Teddy) Roosevelt. He was a Rough Rider and one of the Presidents of the United States of America. It is said that "Teddy" has a place of honor in the home of that loved man.

While we bears lived in Arkansas we all shared a room on the balcony overlooking the happenings in the Great Room below us. I miss my den mates and look forward to the day when they emerge and join me.

We all get stuffed in corners and boxes around December, when we are replaced by all those Nutcrackers, but that is another story for another time. Suffice it to say you will learn more at a later date.

Meanwhile, we bears will share the limelight. Then we will be scattered throughout the house, unceremoniously dumped into boxes that were vacated by all those nutcrackers.

Trust you all picked up on the various ways the word "stuffed" was used.

* * * * * *

THE RIVER
Lea Meadow 11/11/11

I am the River. My journey began before the coming of Man, when Nature ruled the Earth and all was at peace. Where did I begin? And why did the Great Provider feel my presence was necessary.

Man discovered my many attributes early in his journey on this land. It was necessary to drink of my waters, to quench the thirst he felt within, just as the flora and fauna had learned when they were created. The Earth is round and constantly rotating, yet I have my place and remain quite constant in my flow toward the ocean, where the ebb of the tides carry me out to sea.

Continuing the theory that the Earth is round and that there are four poles, which determine the latitude and longitude of Earth, let us surmise that I come from the North and flow South. I possess strength untold that allows me to forge deep canyons and steep mountains.

My path is not always straight, but weaves in and out of the ravines that I encounter. My journey is often rapid, causing me to tumble at great speeds. Sometimes the Creator has unloosed a terrible storm that changes the course of my travels. This is Nature at work, and is nothing that Man in his infinite wisdom has found a means to totally control.

Man has found ways to divert my

wanderings. Dams have been built in an attempt to harness my waters to irrigate his fields.

The Great Provider has developed caverns to contain my nourishment that all living creatures, great and small, require.

My moods are many. Mostly I prefer to rest in quiet repose, allowing the creatures that live within my waters and those who come to drink and sustain themselves with my bountiful attributes. I enjoy their visits, knowing that the Creator will find a way to replenish me.

In the beginning a great Ice Age covered most of the frigid regions of Earth. The cold months would freeze my waters, creating large icebergs, which floated southward, creating larger and deeper ravines, where they met the warm air currents that melted the ice into water.

You live near my body of water that supplies you with much needed sustenance. When Nature provides an overabundance of rain or snow, I will flow over my banks that contain my force. When this happens there is a flood. When left unattended my powers saturated the Earth, which may cause unpleasant things to occur.

You may need my waters for your survival. It is Man's responsibility to protect me from greed and unnecessary abuse. Be kind and responsible in your duties.

* * * * * * *

A MOMENT OF SILENCE
9/11/11

What is "silence?" According to my *American Heritage Dictionary* silence is:

1) The condition or quality of being or keeping silent; avoidance of speech or noise.

2) The absence of sound; stillness.

3) A period of time without speech or noise.

4) Refusal or failure to speak out; secrecy.

What would it be like to have a moment when the second definition was present – "the absence of sound, stillness?"

Even if you were encased in a "soundproof" room, would there be absolute silence – you are alive, you are breathing – but is there silence?

As children, we were truly never silent. Body parts wriggled, brushing something that made a sound, a noise.

We breathe in and out. Air is not silent. We move a leg or an arm, a joint creaks.

Listen to the hush of the woods. A vehicle traveling on the roadway. Trees gently swaying in the breeze. A moment of silence as we bow our heads to pray.

The absolute quiet as we learned of the explosion of the twin towers, stunned for a second, then a reaction settles upon us. Silence no longer.

* * * * * * * * *

REACHING IN PULLING OUT
1/27/09

What's this, I ask myself. Where on Earth did it ever come from and why is it in my writer's case?

I suppose if one was a giant or extremely arthritic, one could possibly use it for writing purposes. But I am not a giant nor extremely arthritic so would have no reason to purchase such an item.

Would it serve any other purpose than that of a writing implement, you ask. It might make a good practical joke. But I am not a practical joker, so I surely would not have purchased it for such a purpose.

It is shaped like a writer's tool. Elongated with a tip and something that resembles a pushing device. It is a hideous bright orange, which would certainly help one find it if it were ever lost. Other than its outrageous size, one could certainly class it as a writing tool.

It is amongst my possessions for now but not

for long. I intend to find its rightful owner who is more than likely at a loss without it. Bless this individual for needing a tool of this size.

* * * * * * * * *

OLD WIVES' TALES
Lea Meadow

We have all had our mother tell us to cover our mouth and nose when we sneeze, so that germs aren't spread to others.

In "The Crowning Glory", found on Wickipedia, "one of the most indestructible parts of the body" is our hair. It further states that someone with "lank" (or long, limp and straight) hair defines one as being of a cunning nature.

While if your hair is curly, you are good natured and full of fun. Long hair denotes strength (e.g. Sampson) and you have luck.

If you prefer to have unlucky hair, by all

means get a haircut when the moon is in the wane, for that phenomenon will cause the hair "to fall out and lose its luster". (This writer would assume that if one's hair fell out, it wouldn't have any luster.)

Cutting your own hair will tempt fate. NEVER pull out gray hairs – for one will be replaced by ten!

From hair we traverse to ear lobes. The greater the lobe, the more intelligent.

Your nose indicates character. A prominent nose shows intelligence and determination. A thin nose may indicate jealousy and uncertainty.

A receding nose will tell us that the wearer has a bad temper and is obstinate. A person with a tip-tilted nose is bright and lively.

But for those readers who have a tendency to bite your tongue while eating, BEWARE. You have recently told a lie and now we all know it!

* * * * * * * * *

A WILD WINTER
Lea Meadow 2/10/12

    The winter of 2011-2012 has been a roller coaster best avoided.

    What began as a mild "leg ulcer" developed into many journeys to the Wound Center in Bloomington, visiting the Neurology offices of IU Medical facilities and daily changes of a bandage to the right ankle, ably performed by Doctor George Thurston, an unlicensed, yet knowledgeable lay person.

    Moving from balmy Arkansas to south western Indiana, it was anticipated that winters would be more like southern Iowa or Connecticut, snow and cold temperatures. So far, it has been a mild winter, a little snow, no gusting winds and temperatures very mild . . . upper twenties to lower forties.

    We can be very thankful for these conditions, as they lent themselves to all those trips to doctors, and even the hospital, where tests were conducted that the doctors' offices were unable to supply.

The prognosis is still pending. Once all the x-rays and tests have been read by knowledgeable medical personnel, life can move forward, sans constant running to a doctor or nurse.

That day cannot come too soon.

* * * * * * * * *

MY PET CAT SNITCHED ON ME
Lea Meadow 2/17/12

How and when elude me, but somewhere in my very experienced, rather lengthy life, my darned cat snitched on me.

My trustworthy *American Heritage Dictionary* defines *snitch: to steal (something of little or no value); to turn informer. Usually used with "on"*. . . So far, so good.

One would surmise that my cat had the ability to use his talents to find an ear to bend with wild stories of *all* the times I had erred and been caught by my erstwhile friend, Cat. Makes me wonder what I did that so offended that darn cat, or for that matter, *which* darn cat, as over all those years I had many cats.   So, we will use our old friend, *Boston Blackie*, a cat with whom my readers have ventured through with other tales of a similar nature. Maybe he heard about the time my first cat, *Tiger*, charmed his way into the lap of my cat-hating father, to share a beer or two. Now, there was a true tomcat, old *Tiger*. But we won't travel that road today, either.

Time for a little history into the ancestry of *Boston Blackie*, whose nickname was "Bee". Bee was the youngest in one of his mother's many litters. His mother was a beautiful cat whose name was *Ethel*. If you were fortunate enough to have been around in the 1960s and heard of the Kennedy clan from The Cape, that cat was named in honor of Robert Kennedy's wife and mother of his numerous offspring. Enough said. Now what could a mere cat "snitch" from or on me, a mere human being? Suffice it to say he "stole our affections." Affections snitched from his admiring human owners. No, sharers of *his* abode, for he definitely ruled the roost!

* * * * * * * * *

SUNSETS HERE AND THERE
Lea Meadow

Having traveled numerous times within these United States, we have seen Eastern sunsets and Western sunsets. As one can ascertain by looking at the pictures, some of these sunsets have been spectacular.

Needless to say, photos of not so spectacular sunsets have not met our camera lens, or vice versa.

If you live in a congested city environment or valley, finding open space to view these sunsets is to your disadvantage. Country living opens all sorts of new experiences, sunsets only a part of them.

In my sojourns across this continent sunsets that truly stand out were found in the Western skies of Arizona and New Mexico as pictures paint scenes that words can only begin to fathom, these would be my parting words: go out, look up and view the skies and the horizon. The marvels are there for all to ponder.

* * * * * * * * *

THE RAGING FIRE
Lea Meadow

One never knows what starts a raging fire. Bonfires in the back yard can become rather awesome, but totally unequal to a smoldering haystack that has lost control. My husband and I were firefighters in another lifetime and have helped to extinguish a number of unforgettable blazes, from structures to purposely set fires for firefighter training.

Exactly why on a particular beautiful spring day this haystack ignited has never been totally explained. Suffice it to say, it happened, probably due to hay that had not been dried thoroughly before the hay binder compacted it for storage.

Damp hay set ablaze transmits an odor and a smoldering that previously to that momentous day had not been observed by the small, but dedicated, small town fire department of which we were members. It stung throats and eyes with a fury of its own. Our clothes and lungs were drenched in that awful stink. We would live to fight other hay bales in our days of firefighting. That one stands out most prominently.

* * * * * * * * * * * * * * * * * *

THE LAST OF THE NUTS
Lea Meadow 3/16/12

Where to go with that one!

Chapter One

Imagine a humanoid has been munching on a bag of walnuts. Needless to say, the shells have been removed. IF one of those nuts fell onto the ground, would it grow? Come on, use the peanut sized brain, scoff and go on with your life.

NOW, imagine you are a totally different species of nut trees, like an Oak. Oaks produce acorns. Human types are not prone to devouring acorns. Ah, but how about Squirrels . . . now we are talking major lunch snacks.

Mr. Squirrel fills his rather abundant cheeks with his find, and heads home to his nest, of course, in the same tree, uses his strong jaws and cracks that nut. Yummy. Not to me, but to the squirrel.

And so the story goes.

Chapter Two

I have been pondering my life, where I have been, where I am and where this all could lead. Today is sunny. Tonight the moon shall be full. Oops. Full moon. Another chapter.

We know the world is full of human nuts. But do we desire to be classified as one of that type? You've seen them all. Some wear kooky clothing. Some wear none.

You see one and say, "Look at that NUT!", shake your head and move on. Of course, there you walk in your plaid pants and striped shirt, and this other "Nut" says to himself . . . you get the picture. Which category do I fit? I will leave that up to you.

Chapter Three

It was the last nut of the season. Jack and Jill had gone home with their pail full of nuts. The squirrel decided his nest was full, and hibernated with his stash. The nut remained on the ground under a warm layer of leaves, swelling with anticipation, while its roots sprouted and reached for the soil to become a seedling, then a young tree. When Mother Nature decided it was time, fruit followed and the cycle once more begins.

Thus I am born. A nut that would eventually find its way to the Super Market, where another humanoid takes it home, turns on the TV and devours said Nut.

Such is life.

* * * * * * * * *

WHO'S IN MY NAME?
Lea Meadow

My Very Early Years

June 27, 1934 . . . or was it June 26? The official birth certificate from the State of South Dakota has a flaw. It reads "Nancy Jane Voss", but someone wrote over the 26, changing it to 27, or was it 27 changed to 26? My baby book, in Mother's handwriting, says it was the 27th at 9 p.m., so we will go by that, as "Mother knows best"! Regardless, I was born, the second daughter to Elizabeth Arp and Ernest Voss at McKennan Hospital in Sioux Falls, South Dakota.

My mother said it was hot that day and the fans were buzzing. The American Legion fife and drum corps was practicing under the window for two hours, preparing for the Fourth of July celebration. She also wrote in my baby book that these circumstances made them decide "she ought to be a hot tamale"! I'm not too sure it was ever the case, but I can attest to the fact that I helped create some tense moments during the years that followed! We stayed in the hospital for twelve days, an unheard of precedence today, and drove home in "our 1929 Chevrolet".

One fond memory of that Chevrolet was on a rare trip to visit Grandmother Voss in Lakefield, Minnesota. It was winter and sister, Jimmy, and I shared the back seat of the car, wrapped snuggly under a woolen blanket. I was wearing my black satin coat which my mother had quilted, lined and sewn, two adorable handmade dresses, one of pink silk and the other crocheted in peach cotton thread, from my early years. However, my first "trip" was Labor Day, 1934 when we went to Lakefield. This would have been the annual gathering of the Voss clan to celebrate the birthday of Grandmother Voss, who was born September 1, 1859. I rode in style in my "car basket" that had been a birth present from Aunt Mid. I also went to McKennan Park in a carriage borrowed from the son of Mother's friend, Mrs. Parr, which got a fresh coat of paint. During warm summer days, this trek to the park became a daily outing, where we watched Jimmy "swim" and where we had lots of picnics. I remember that "pool" in the park, a rather glorified wading pool and a good water sport start for all three sisters!

Baby books, like family Bibles and diaries, are a great source of information from times before our memory is fully developed. My name took "three or more days of wavering between Barbara, Marian and Nancy. If she grows up to be dignified she can call herself <u>Jane</u>". Mother always said it was fortunate that they did NOT name me Grace, as graceful I never became! In fairness to all, however, she must not have realized that the name, Nancy, is a variant of Ann from Hebrew, which means "grace".

Being a Wednesday's child, I *may* have been "full of woe", or "have far to go", or "loving and giving". There are a number of variations regarding the poetry of the seven days of the week. My parents, siblings and offspring will all have different interpretations.

The baby book also states that I cut my first tooth in Luverne, Minnesota while chewing hard on "Aunt Mid's Tinker Toy dog"! This was December 16, 1934. At four years of age, I lost a molar, but the remaining baby teeth were "still intact". Mother says I never crept very much, but used to "sit up and hitch herself over the floor". I talked very little, "we all talk for her too much" and my first sentence came when I was "almost seventeen months of age". Just smile and sit on your little round keister, the world will come to you!

Introduction to the high chair first occurred on December 10, 1934. This was probably the same high chair that allegedly tipped over while I was being the "doll" to my sister, Jimmy, and her friends. No serious damage to either chair or occupant, thank you.

Eventually , there would be three daughters born to Betty and Ern, for those were the names they went by, then and until their deaths. The oldest daughter was named Virginia Elizabeth, and was always and forever called "Jimmy" . . . probably because Ern always figured he would father boys, not girls! Jimmy was almost eleven years my senior and the apple of everyone's eye. Must have been a shock to suddenly have a baby sister.

Jimmy and her friends soon adopted me, as I became their living, breathing doll! Gave Mom a chance to rest up from the big event, which was big, in all ways, as I was a month late, or so the story goes, and weighed in at eight and one half pounds. All that sitting around in the shelter of the womb did wonders for my girlish figure!

I had no hair . . . zilch . . . but big blue eyes and a smile a mile wide. The hair came much later, blonde and curly. I was the only blonde in the Ernest Richard Voss household, which always intrigued me as a child. I loved to fantasize about being adopted. I was a chubby little girl for the first three years. I was also a very slow learner when it came to walking. Why walk, for heaven's sake, when thirty-nine thousand adults were more than willing to be at my beck and call? Just a real big smile and the world was my oyster.

My mother was a frail woman who should never have had children. The pregnancies were hard for her. She virtually spent the last three months of that pregnancy in bed. Memory says she was extremely toxic. Grandma Arp, her mother came to stay with us until after my birth.

This upset my two aunts, Mildred and Gladys, who felt that their mother was too ill herself to care for their sister and niece. I have a letter from Gladys to brother Harry, which proves this statement. However, Grandma came, Grandma stayed, and I have an adorable picture of the two of us that shows the joy in both our faces . . . me and my bald head and chubby body, Grandma with the girth of what we always associated came with old age!

We lived in a small "cottage" in those days. Daddy was one of nine children born to Hans and Catherine Voss, farmers through and through.

Somehow farming was not in Ernie's genetic heritage, and upon marriage, he opted for the city life. When Jimmy hit the scene on October 31, 1923, the Vosses were in Sioux Falls, South Dakota on acreage that Grandpa Hans had purchased for them, as part of the Voss heritage, and was definitely "out in the country" at the time. So, a small two bedroom cottage grew, and the vegetable garden with it. Not to mention the "four leaf clovers" which were an obsession with Ern. And he could find those suckers, too!

I was a depression baby, a time in the history of our country that was dreaded by those old enough to know what it was all about. Being just a babe, I only reaped the love of my family, growing up without a care in the world.

"Hide and Go Seek" was a favorite game played by Mother and Daughter. We were very close in those early years. Jimmy was off to school, Ernie busy making a living for his little clan, selling and laying carpet and linoleum, a career he followed until his retirement after attaining 70 years of age. We had plenty of time to bond.

We *girls* did what mothers and daughters did. We played, we cleaned, we rested, and we laughed . . . a lot. New words entered the vocabulary while playing "Hide and Go Seek". *"Hoy, hoy"* was the preferred vernacular, used by both.

My favorite hiding places were in the cupboard in the corner behind the pots and pans and the "root cellar". Now that was an awesome place. It had a black wooden door, a dirt floor and not much headspace. When you entered the rear door of our home, the basement steps were to your left. The root cellar was directly in front of you, and to the right were three of four steps that led to the main part of the house. Above the back door stood the Ice Box, a fancy concoction that held the vital food elements, such as Milk, Butter and Eggs. And a huge block of ice to keep it all cool and fresh! Other than affording me with a great hiding place, the "root cellar" held all the other great food items, such as potatoes, carrots and onions. There were also any number of spider webs and other creatures of the dark, which in those days didn't faze me in the least. I was also known to eat my share of garden-variety bugs and worms!

Back to the ice. In the mid-1930s those less fortunate families relied on the old-fashioned "ice box" to keep the perishables. We had electricity, but it was a dear commodity, used sparingly. As I grew a little older, I remember the trips with Daddy to the Ice House to pick up this block of coldness. It was strapped to the bumper of the car, and on hot summer days you would leave a trail of melted ice on the street where your automobile traversed.

All in all, my early childhood was a time of pleasure. I loved to play in my sand pile, make mud/sand pies, play with my grungy brown teddy bear and invite Mother to a tea party.

Further Adventures from the Early Years

I don't recollect a lot about my older sister during my early years. Jimmy was almost eleven years my senior. I have photographs of her with Daddy and Mother. She actually called them "Ern" and "Betty", as we went where our parents went, such as Bridge and Poker Games with their friends. Baby-sitters were not within our budget in those Depression Days. As Jimmy always heard them addressed as "Ern" and "Betty", it was an easy step to apply those monikers. I always called Mother "Mother" and Father "Daddy". Always, to this day.

Jimmy and I shared a small bedroom in those early days. There was room for a double bed and a dresser. We shared a walk-in closet with the folks. It divided the two bedrooms, with walk-through doors. Thinking about it, that was another of my favorite hiding places. Mother wore formal dresses frequently. The folks loved to dance. Mother's long dresses afforded me a niche on the shoe rack where I could hide.

The most memorable occasion I have is when I came down with some horrible malady, probably chicken pox or scarlet fever, which isolated the family from intruders. A large <u>*Quarantined*</u> sign was hung on the front door to keep away unsuspecting individuals. Daddy brought me a whole case of *Orange Crush*, which sat at the foot of the bed. What a treat.

There were exciting times growing up in our private little *country* setting. I wasn't aware of it then, and was never told specifically, but the land that Ern inherited from his father, Hans, was more extensive than a city lot. It probably covered a couple acres, for during the decades that followed, it would be subdivided several times.

Before daughter three joined us in 1939, Mother and I were alone most of the day.

From the kitchen window as you looked past the driveway, a cornfield stood. Across the street were other cornfields. And "things" inhabited those fields. Primarily, they had two legs and looked much like Mother and me. Except their clothing was "far-out" as the saying goes.

These people were *GYPSIES*. Nomads who roamed from place to place. I was even allowed to be outdoors and to play with the children. Until *THE DAY* when Mother and I witnessed a very bad scene in that cornfield. A man was murdered, with a knife, I do believe. Mother and I were sitting at the kitchen table, having a mid-morning snack.

A big commotion arose from across the tall

cornstalks. I remember we girls put our heads down on the table until all was clear. And that was the end of the Gypsies never to be seen or heard from again in our cornfield.

I loved to play outdoors. There was a big old apple tree in the back yard and under it was my sandbox. I would take my Teddy Bear and dolls to my other world, and we would bake many, many cakes and such in the sand. When my cakes were all baked, I would invite Mother to join us for cake and tea, all properly served on my best China. Such fun!

Another great adventure was the *HAIL STORM*. When it hailed, we didn't count the little occurrences, just the major events. Daddy and Jimmy ran outside, with me on their heels, to retrieve the softball size hail stones.

They were placed in the Ice Box for future viewing.

* * * * * * * * * * * * * * * * *

EMILY CADY
Lea Meadow

Gazing at the lovely sampler hanging on my wall, I awoke to the realization that I actually didn't know much about it or of the young girl who lovingly stitched it. Who was Emily Cady and why did I have her sampler, dated 1816? I know it has been in the family for several generations. It hung on my mother's wall all the time I was growing up. She got it from her mother, my grandmother Katy.

So, I went to the internet, a blessed invention that has helped me so much the past five years while searching for my family roots. In my favorite genealogy site, *ancestry.com*, I entered the name "Emily Cady" in the search area, with one result, a marriage in New York to a Thomas Knapp.

The truth hit me like a modern day marvel! This was my mother's grandmother's maiden name, and Emily Cady would have been my great-great grandmother!

And so began the fantasy of the girl, Emily Cady:

Emily Cady woke to the damp, dark morning. She had just turned ten, but was already wise beyond her years.

Her brother, Grisham, four years her senior, slept peacefully in the bunk above her in the small log cabin her father, Palmer, had built shortly before Grisham was born in 1802.

It was December and Emily was already looking forward to Christmas and the gift her mother, Rhoda, was busy making for her. Emily knew it would be something to treasure. Mother was teaching Emily to read and write and do simple needlework. Emily was proud of the sampler she was secretly doing, and hoped that she would have it finished to give her mother on Christmas!

Grisham tossed gently above her, then stretched and jumped from his perch. The loft was exceedingly cold and drafty. Pa would demand his presence in the stable shortly, so he dressed rapidly. Gresham poked Emily, and enjoyed keeping his little sister under his watchful eye. "Get up, Emily, the chickens are hungry and the eggs will freeze in their nests if you don't get moving!", Grisham chided. "There's more to life than doing fancy needlework, you know". How she hated dressing to face the new day out in the cold, cold barn, where the only heat was generated from the beasts living there. Being in the kitchen with Ma, baking bread and stitching on her sampler was more appealing to this petite, fragile girl!

I pondered what to do with Emily. While collecting my wandering thoughts, I went to my own kitchen and proceeded to put together a loaf of delectable whole wheat bread, kneading it just as my mother had taught me as a girl, a trade that more than likely had been handed down from mother to mother for so many generations.

Where did Emily live, when did she marry and how many children did she bear? All were thoughts that went through my head as I kneaded that bread. So back to my fantasy: Emily grew up to be a very talented young lady. Palmer and Rhoda Cady were proud of their children, Emily and Gresham.

They had lived and farmed in rural upper New York, about 85 miles north of New York City. Palmer had been born right there in Columbia County in 1799, shortly after the United States had declared the thirteen colonies as states and had established counties. Rhoda was six years his junior and a fine housekeeper and teacher.

"Emily, dear, clear the cobwebs from your mind and help me with the stitching of the lace on your wedding gown," Rhoda chided her daughter. "Thomas will not wait forever to marry you just because your gown is not finished."

It was a beautiful day in May, 1828, when Emily became the bride of Thomas Sheldon Knapp. He was a dashing young man of 27 and his young bride was five years his junior. His first wife had died in childbirth when their son, George, was born in 1826. Emily was their neighbor and had helped Thomas raise the boy. It was only natural that they would marry.

Young George was seven years of age before he was joined by his first brother, young Thomas Cogswell. Emily enjoyed their sons, but longed for a daughter to share the household chores. This longing would continue for a number of years, while three more boys joined the family circle.

In 1845 little Clarissa brightened the day. Emily could now pass along her skills in the kitchen and around the loom! How sad the family were at the abrupt passing of this fragile little babe in her first year. The appearance of little Martha in 1847 helped to ease the pain. She would be the last child born to Emily and Thomas. Amazingly, Martha would endure growing up with all those male siblings and remain the apple of her parent's eyes!

Thankfully, my quest for Emily had allowed me the opportunity to become acquainted with this wonderful ancestor. Now when I gaze upon the sampler, I have a renewed feeling of kinship with my great-great grandmother. Bless her.

* * * * * * * * * * * * * * * * *

A JOB NOBODY WANTED
Lea Meadow

I worked as a dispatcher for the Cherokee Village Volunteer Fire Department in Arkansas for over five years. No one wanted to work from 11 p.m. to 7 a.m. Being the new kid on the block, that was my assignment.

I wasn't there very long before the knowledge of its unacceptability became very obvious. The firefighters on duty were all snoring away, the phone forgot how to ring and the boredom loomed long and hard.

Kelly, one of the on-duty overnight firefighters, introduced me to computer games.

Solitaire soon became boring, so we ventured out to other games attainable, such as Free Cell and Spider. These games became addictive and still occupy much of my "free" time, time that could be well spend pursuing the trail leading to my ancestors across eastern Germany (then more likely a part of Prussia), following them through a brief stay in Indiana before settling in southwest Minnesota.

There were four dispatchers who shared the responsibility of dispatching one of the four stations which encompassed the rather spread out area of Cherokee Village. It was important to find the location of the fire in order to dispatch the proper truck or trucks, depending on the size and type of the incident. Sometimes it would be a grass fire, but the ones that were dreaded involved a structure.

Arkansas is not so far south that winter conditions do not exist. Roads can be very hazardous, with severe blizzards, icy conditions on hilly, curving roads. Firefighters are trained for all types of fires and weather phenomenon. I lived about 16 miles east of the fire station. Like the postal service, regardless of the weather I was hired to appear on time, ready to serve my community. I never missed my shift, and sometimes covered a double shift . . . once even three shifts! Dedication? Maybe not. Possibly more an attitude, why not? I was there anyhow, and no one else wanted the job! Needless to say, I racked up some pretty serious overtime.

One of my fellow dispatchers (we were all women) lived in a more remote area than I did, at least as far away. Her husband was a firefighter. The premise being, if he could make it to work, so could she. I lived on a better highway, so could I! So we did. It was our job and if nobody else was dedicated (or foolish) we obliged. When the firemen on duty finally fell asleep, those nights could become very long and exhausting.

Once in a while, one of the men on security patrol would come by to stretch his legs and grab a cup of very strong, very stale coffee and chat for a while. I could read or play solitaire just so long, and my eyes would close. Not for long, as anyone who has tried to sleep sitting up will attest, the neck will stiffen and joints will jolt you awake.

There was only one incident where I refused to drive the long, winding road from the highway into the Village. One of the firefighters came to the highway and drove me back to the station, not in a fire truck, but in his own personal SUV.

It always amazed me that one of my fellow dispatchers couldn't find it in her means to trek the extra six miles from her house to mine, one of the reasons why I got the overtime.

I liked the work and the fellowship. Although it was a job nobody wanted, it was a good job. I learned a lot about firefighting and endurance. The job did not stop me from joining our little town of Williford, putting out fires in my home community.

* * * * * * * * * * * * * * * * * *

NIGHT SOUNDS
Lea Meadow

Hush

Listen to the sounds of the night
Whoooo . . .whoooo . . .whoo
The owl in the willow repeats
Whishhh . . . whishhh . . .whishh
Tires speed by on the wet tar road
Too fast . . . too fast . . . they go

Everyone in a hurry
Going fast, getting nowhere
Where to go . . . where to go
These are the signs of the open road.
Toot, toot, toot
Taxis slipping in and out
Traffic heading here and there

Where have the occupants been
Where are they going
Why must they go so fast

Bumpers colliding
Tempers flaring
Horns blasting

These are the sounds of the city night.

* * * * * * * * * * * * * * * *

STOP THAT NOISE
Lea Meadow

If you have ever worked the graveyard shift, you will appreciate this little ditty. Working overnight, sleeping by day was not the easiest job I ever held. Dogs bark, cats meow, and children scream while they play out of doors. Not to mention all the noises that birds make while building nests or feeding those chirping youngsters.

When my babies were young, nighttime always brought forth joyous, raucous noises from the nursery. The first child, a little girl, had colic. She could sleep away daytime hours like a charm, but darkness brought forth the bellyaches, the crying and the screams. Only a cushion of mother's shoulder, the gentle pats on the back, would soothe the savage beast that tormented her innards. So we walked the floor, wore out the rocking chair, and survived.

Many years later, memories of those sleepless nights had all but faded. I was a dispatcher for the local fire department. It was my duty to keep an ear tuned to the radio, while the firefighters on duty peacefully slept, some snoring . . . others passing the hours in silence. Those nights became intolerably long and lonely. Reading was a short time endeavor, for the book would suddenly leap from my hands, crashing to the counter, jolting me awake. So I played solitaire on the computer, a very addictive and seductive pastime that has plagued me all these years.

* * * * * * * * *

AN OBJECT IN THE ROAD AHEAD
Lea Meadow

I have traveled many roads in my lifetime. Most of them have led me to better times, places. I never purposely walked backward in time, never had a desire to try to change what went before, just improve the road that lies ahead.

One cannot alter what happened in the past, but try not to make the same mistakes over again. If the road did not take you where you should have been, take another road. On a less philosophical path, I will recount some of the roads taken that have led me to the course pursued. These are true happenings along life's path, pretty much in chronological order, some decidedly humorous, few if any sad.

I learned to drive at the tender age of thirteen. My father was a patient man, the sire of three girls. He wanted boys, and after three girls decided, enough is enough. We sisters were spaced out through the years. Virginia Elizabeth was eleven years my senior, I survived infancy as the living doll of her and her friends. Margaret Ann followed me five years later, a definite "change of life" for our mother.

I came along in 1934. In 1939 we moved up from the 1922 Studebaker, to a late 1930's model. The war came along and new vehicles were taboo, as the metal was needed to make equipment that transported the Army, Navy and Marines around the world. So during the lengthy war years, it was decided to add a new coat of paint and keep going, if only the short distance to work and Sunday school. Paint was applied by hand, by brush. There weren't any fancy detail shops in those days.

The old Studebaker saw us through the war years, when it was replaced by a parade of Studebakers until driving stopped for daddy. I kept the tradition alive with a 1949 Studebaker that was shaped in such a manner that it was rather difficult to determine whether it was going forward or backward.

However, this story is entitled "the object in the road ahead," so enough diversion.

The first object in the road ahead had four legs and just stood there in the middle of the road. Daddy assumed that if he got me onto a country road, the wheel could be transferred to me. That was fine and dandy, UNTIL there was an obstacle in the middle of the road. "Daddy, what shall I do?" I nervously inquired. The response was a suggestion that I honk my horn. If the obstacle, which had four legs and resembled a cow, didn't respond to the honking of the horn, I would just have to go around it, which is what I did.

Another time, many years later, another object crossed the road, stopping in the middle of the road in the Grand Canyon National Park, very near the visitor's center. He was a big bull moose and it was HIS domain. So everyone grabbed cameras, got out of the vehicles and took pictures, while he politely posed and when too bored, moved on. That was a fun time!

Buffalo are big. Buffalo who decide to have lunch where you have parked to enjoy your own meal can be a challenge. They have no concept of time, or so it seems. So they just graze along, contentedly chewing and chewing, while you just sit there, waiting for a clear road to continue down your journey. OR, they will just graze right in the middle of the only road in and out of the spot you decided to mistakenly make a wrong turn.

Understand, the Rangers in the national and state parks are only too happy and well trained NOT to mention to motorists that the herd is in a certain area within the park. If you wish to observe them, you should follow a certain path, but not try to come between the herd, which is grazing on the other side of the road.

My sister, who has a lovely summer home in the Black Hills of South Dakota, graciously took my cousin and myself to see these magnificent beasts in their natural surroundings. We stopped the car, rolled down some windows and pointed the cameras in the right direction. All well and good, unless you are a city girl, as is our cousin, who wanted a closer look. Before she could be stopped, the car door opened, Kate got out with her camera in hand, and snapped pictures, while we sat in the car, mouths agape, just wishing she would get back in the car before being gored. Fortunately, her presence went undetected . . . lunch amongst the blades of grass more delectable than human flesh.

These are some of the more obvious objects in the road ahead. The others are philosophical and too profound to discuss in such a forum as this. Life has many obstacles we must overcome, but not objects that are worthy of discussion amongst fellow writers. Leave them for the couch and the doctor's office.

* * * * * * * * *

HABITS TO LIVE BY
Lea Meadow

There are good and bad habits. We all acquire some of both types, but presumably one would prefer to live by good habits.

Habits are generally acquired through several avenues: we are taught by our elders the preferred way to live through their examples and/or admonishes. It may be assumed that the preference would be to acquire and live by GOOD habits.

Good habits could (and should) include our personal hygiene: brush your teeth, comb your hair, clean underwear (at least, wear underwear). This habit was instilled to me by mother at a very young age.

My mother wore a girdle, the old-fashioned kind that had not crotch, with garters that held up her silk stockings. My thinking went along the lines that if Mother did not wear underpants, then why should I. She was quite aghast when I sat in the chair legs apart and NO underpants. Her premise on the donning of underpants, "What if you were involved in an accident and it was discovered that you were quite naked under those beautiful over-garments? God forbid!" So I wore underpants, always.

Other good habits should include politeness to others, no matter their demeanor toward you. "Hey, teach" was not an appropriate manner to address your educators. Hands were always raised (not waved) to get the teacher's attention, who may or may not necessarily heed your eagerness to answer ALL the questions. Thirty other eager, bright students needed their turn to shine.

One should not come to the supper table (or

any other table where food is served) with grimy hands or dirty mouths. Soap and water were required on exposed body parts before you sat down.

I once was a member of a writer's group where another member wrote a delightful book entitled "Naked Ears". She repeatedly heard her mother tell her to wash her "naked ears" before coming to the table. Her problem was that she could not understand why her ears were naked.

A habit I began many years ago came about from a dislocated rotator cuff and involves daily exercises to alleviate pain for it and a stiff neck. It is a ritual that I have continued every day, rain, shine, at home or away. None of them are extremely zealous, and are performed sitting on the edge of the bed. They are stretching exercises for neck, arms and legs. Only after that has been accomplished do I wander to the kitchen for another indulgence . . . a big mug of freshly brewed coffee.

I once went to a doctor to find out why I always suffer from a stiff neck. Whether he was being facetious or honest, I will never know, but he informed me that I do NOT have a stiff neck, for if I did it would be next to impossible to turn it side to side or up and down. So much for stiff necks! Frankly, I don't care for his assessment . . . I do have a stiff neck and shoulders, they bother me most of the time and to alleviate the discomfort, I indulge in a habit I deplore, I take an Aleve or Advil. It works, so I indulge. Guess it really does not make me a druggie!

An indulgence that I love involves a cat. He doesn't have fur, but a nice cloth covering over his therapeutic stuffing. For best results he is placed in the microwave for a minute or so and then stretched across your neck, while you sit in your comfortable chair, reading or doing a crossword puzzle (other habits that are nightly rituals). These are better done while consuming a dish of ice cream, which is one of the less desirable habits acquired, but so very welcome.

Good habits, bad habits, habits we tolerate and live by or with. My "Complete Word Finder" tells me a habit is 1) a settled or regular tendency or practice; 2) a practice that is hard to give up; 3) a mental constitution or attitude. We all have them.

* * * * * * * * *

MY FEELINGS ON THE ROAD TO RECOVERY
Lea Meadow

My advice to those who dream: keep it simple, keep it calm and don't fall out of bed.

The doctor recently diagnosed me with "early onset of Alzheimer's" and prescribed me with medication, which she said MIGHT cause me to have weird dreams. Some definitions of "dreams" and "weird" probably should have been explained to me in great detail. I can certainly attest to having dreams and in my humble opinion, weird is a mild adjective to use.

One morning I awoke thudding to the floor when a wild animal was chasing me. I have been on the road to recovery ever since . . . at least ten days (or nights) later. The fall wasn't so bad, but an old adage states that it isn't the fall but the landing that hurts.

It is my uneducated opinion that one should not have dreams that in reality have the dreamer land on the floor, any floor. The tops of my toes on the left foot were all bruised, thus it is likely that the toes were the first area to hit the floor.

This poses an interesting question: if one falls out of bed on the right side of the bed, why would the toes on the left side of the body be victims of that fall? Hmmm.

We do enjoy a dish of ice cream before retiring for the night. I do not recollect seeing anything on a carton of ice cream that states weird dreams may occur when eating this delicious bedtime snack. Or maybe it is the combination of the ice cream and the consuming of the alleged "dream" pill that triggers the dreams.

The doctor says I need the medication, my tummy cries out for the ice cream, so the dreams will more than likely persist.

SLED RIDE OF WINTER
Lea Meadow

When we were growing up in Sioux Falls, South Dakota, our new home had about a six-inch rise from the house lot proper and the balance of the property. As I was just a youngster of eight, this was enough challenge for me to take my small sled for a dip down the hill! Up and down I would travel until my cheeks were rosy and I had physically had enough.

As an adult I had occasion to visit Jackson, Minnesota, where my mother had spent a great deal of time as a child. Her father was Superintendent of Schools for Jackson County and a newly consolidated school had been build, where his office was located. Jackson has some pretty good-sized hills, similar to that located east of Spencer on the way to Bloomington. This is where she, her older brother and maybe the younger sisters spent winter months sledding up and down the hill not far from their home. It must have been an exhilarating slide down,an awesome walk back to the top to do it all over again. Certainly nothing like my little incline in Sioux Falls.

Growing up our home was located where the street in front ran down a short hill before it stopped where the new Catholic Schools were erected. Fourth Avenue was not extremely busy in those early years, and afforded my older sister, Jimmy (eleven years my senior) and me an excellent opportunity to sled to our hearts' content. Adventures with Jimmy will be a chapter in my family biography itself. There were many over the years.

* * * * * * * * *

MY LONGEST DAY
Lea Meadow June 2012

Long days don't always begin at sunrise. My first child was not overly eager to meet the new world. I visited my doctor on December 26 when he advised that the birth was still in the future.

However my Mother flew from Sioux Falls, South Dakota to Long Island, New York on the 26th and advised that the baby would be born the next day! What a surprise! When I awoke the next morning, my water broke, a tell tale sign of things to begin. We called the doctor, who advised that I should take my time, take Mother and husband to lunch and the doctor would meet me at the hospital around mid afternoon. Upon arrival at Flower Fifth Avenue Hospital where this great occasion would happen, the staff was limited . . . there was a strike involving the nurses.

We were shown to our room. I was to have a roommate, a sick roommate suffering from pneumonia. It was not an easy birth, stitches were required and my stay was a long five days. It was a long day.

When I married George, my second husband, it was a beautiful early summer day in the Berkshires of Massachusetts. My dearest friend and neighbor made the wedding cake, a beautiful carrot cake, which the bride and groom to be were to pick up on the way to the ceremony. We were married on top of a beautiful hill at the farm of another of my dear friend's father, at 2:00 pm on June 27, 1981. My daughter (the same as mentioned above) was my maid-of-honor, the best man was a dear friend of both bride and groom and my sons, George's five children, his parents and sister were there to watch the big event.

After indulging in cake and opening the lovely gifts, we climbed into the *Pontiac Firebird* for a honeymoon at the home of another friend in upstate New York. It was a working honeymoon, as it was our duty to house-sit their large setter, who was so glad to see us that he affectionately slobbered all over us. The journey to this honeymoon retreat was LONG; it was midnight before we arrived. I kept assuring the groom "it's just around the next comer, or the next or the next. But eventually it was THE corner. It was a long day.

There have been other long days throughout the years, but those two were without a doubt the longest.

* * * * * * * * *

THE DEER HUNT
Lea Meadow June 2012

It was a very, very cold December morning in Mt. Washington, Massachusetts as the two hunters set off on a quest for the acquisition of one male deer, which was the number and sex listed on their permit. Fortunately the men had the foresight to pack a thermos of hot coffee before they left the house. They arrived at their destination shortly before sunrise, armed themselves with their rifles and waited for a deer to approach. They continued to wait, consuming the coffee in an effort to remain in a semi-thawed state of body and mind.

Deer have an acute sense of the enemy, which in this case was our two stalkers, and were wise to keep their distance. After enduring the biting cold for as long as they could, they packed up their empty thermos, slung their guns over their shoulders and headed back to the parking lot where they had left their car. Standing before them was the prettiest doe eyes could behold.

Should they risk taking her down, with no idea where a game warden might be in ambush, waiting for some fool to fire that weapon? Deciding the risk was more than they wished to take, they climbed into the vehicle and headed for home.

Like the fisherman who liked to exaggerate the size of the one that got away, relating their adventure to anyone with an ear to listen, they recounted their long, cold experience on the crest of Mt. Washington.

* * * * * * * * *

PICTURES OF MY LIFE
Lea Meadow June 2012

I was the middle child, different in so many ways. My parents both had dark hair and blue eyes, as did my sisters. I was a blonde, very, very blonde, curly-haired child. But that came later, as I was born bald.

When I was eight years old, my father's brother, Jack, surprised my parents by taking me shopping for a pretty new dress. It was red with tiny white roses. It was something very special, as Mother was an accomplished seamstress, and made all our dresses and underwear, including underpants and sleepwear. Uncle Jack not only bought me a new dress, patent leather shoes and fancy socks, but also took me to the hairdresser for a perm! My already springy, bouncy naturally curly ringlets were extra bouncy. Both Uncle Jack and I survived Mother's dismay and life went on.

Mother was proud of my name. She had considered naming me "Grace," but always stated that she did NOT regret choosing "Nancy," for I was not in the least way a graceful child. However, if she had consulted the dictionary, or wherever one finds proper names, she would have learned that "Nancy" is the French equivalent for "Grace."

Our neighborhood consisted of many more boys than girls. In an effort to blend in, I learned to play rough, basketball and football included in games that we played. I was of an era that preceded the wearing of "pants" or "slacks," so that when I was outdoors I wore a dress. One day Mother looked out the kitchen window to observe her darling daughter plummet into a rose bush while chasing a ball. I was promptly called home, spanked and sent to my room.

Another neighborhood activity included participating in track running. As I had long legs and was quick on my feet, the boys gave me the honor of leading the team up and down the sidewalks as the "pacer," a challenge I was willing to accept.

When I was old enough to see over the steering wheel of the 1939 Chevrolet, Daddy took me out in the country for my first driving experience. This was the country, dotted with farms and open fields. In front of me, right in the middle of the road, stood a cow. "Daddy, what shall I do?" I nervously queried. His reply, "stop." Needless to say, I stopped the car and waited for Bossy to cross the road.

That old 1939 Chevy saw us through the war years, for our nation was engaged in fighting on two fronts: Germany on the European field and Japan in the Pacific, off the coast of Hawaii, which was not the 50th state of the union, just one of the many islands we invaded to protect our vulnerable west coast. During those war years, Daddy and I even painted that old Chevy, with a brush, battleship gray. She was really something.

We survived the war, suffered standing in line for groceries and other necessities. One line I really remember was waiting for the very precious hosiery, made of synthetics, such as rayon and nylon, as silk was used to make the many parachutes, which enabled our military to penetrate behind "enemy lines". Children today have no conceivable idea of standing in such a line. A close resemblance would be the checkout counter at Wal-Mart. On weekends our living room floor resembled a battlefield of its own. My parents were both involved in the USO. We had an array of soldiers from the local Army base that spent time enjoying some home-cooked meals and Hunting with Ernie, my dad.

Meat was expensive, if available, but

pheasant required a short jaunt into the country, some ammo for the shotguns and a little luck. (Shotgun pellets by the way, can wreak havoc with your teeth, if not carefully extricated by the cook in advance). Maybe that's where the expression "lead in my pants" really originated.

We survived. Other conflicts have touched our lives, but not with the closeness of those war years. There was no television in those days. We huddled around the Philco radio, tuned out the static as best we could, to listen to Paul Harvey tell "the rest of the story," read Ernie Pyle in the newspapers, and got second hand reports on the fighting in fields we never dreamed existed.

I have been married twice. The first time was a fiasco, in the many years endured, produced three lovely children and many gray hairs. The second marriage, going into its thirty-first year, has been such a pleasure, a much better way to spend the Golden Years.

Some of my ancestors crossed Indiana on their way West to Minnesota. In many ways, I feel that moving to this Hoosier state has been like "coming home". The song, "Back Home Again in Indiana" runs through my mind on many occasions. It's good to be "back home".

* * * * * * * * *

MY MOST EMBARRASSING MOMENT
Lea Meadow June 2012

I have lived enough decades to have more than one most embarrassing moment, so I will relate two of them. They both occurred in the Great State of New York. We resided in the nice, quiet village of Belmore, Long Island, New York. I was traveling down the road when a rather upset officer of the law stopped me. He began writing me a ticket for going through a red light. "Officer," I quickly responded, "the light was orange and I had the option of continuing as I had already reached the intersection."

"Please get out of your vehicle, now, and show me this 'orange' light." New York City and suburbs don't have traffic lights with the option of 'orange'. Whether he felt pity for my ignorance or just was not in the mood to write the ticket, I am not sure. He cautioned me to be more observant, and we both went our separate ways.

After enduring five long years of "city" living, I decided it was time to move to the country in neighboring Massachusetts. It was a cold, raw January morning when I bundled the three youngsters into the old Ford station wagon for the long, treacherous ride into the boonies. Cindy was in her "other world" and John and Michael were picking on each other in the back seat, when another diligent officer of the law put on his siren and flashing lights to pull me over. "Lady, your license plate has expired. I need to see your driver's license. Please step out of your vehicle." Two young male voices promptly began to wail.

"Don't take my mother to jail," wailed John. Children can be blessings in disguise that one would never imagine, nor could one train, to put on an act like that. I explained to the trooper that we were moving permanently to Massachusetts, where I would immediately get Massachusetts plates and a Massachusetts driver's license. He still wrote the ticket (probably silently assuming I would never pay) and we went on our merry way. I did NOT pay that ticket, but did go to the Registry of Motor Vehicles as soon as we got settled into our new digs, which were anything but new, as it was an old carriage house, a story of its own.

About five years later, when the children were safely off to school, I went to work as a customer service manager at *Zayres*, where I remained until the store closed. A Registry officer was in the parking lot, writing tickets for various infractions of the law. He wrote me up for having bald tires. I then went into the local Registry to read them the riot act for ticketing people in a public parking lot. The Superintendent, Mr. Gray, read me the riot act for my behavior. When *Zayres* closed, I worked at the State Department of Human Services, helping other unemployed people find employment. When that contract expired, I was given the option of working at the Registry of Motor Vehicles. My new Registry boss shook his head and laughed that I had the utter gall to work under the auspices of the very same man, Mr. Gray, who had so caustically affronted me for breaking the law. I just shrugged, spent five years greeting Mr. Gray, and helped other unsuspecting motorists overcome the wrath of the law.

* * * * * * * * *

SUNSHINE
Lea Meadow 6/29/12

As I sit here pondering the concept of putting into words a connotation or perception of the word "sunshine" the sky is overcast with patches of sunshine in the atmosphere. However, I would hesitate to call it a sunny day.

"Sunshine on my window makes me happy," as the lyrics to an old favorite tune go through my mind. "To bask in the sun" is another phrase. To write about sunshine in any poetic text would be an affront to Robert Frost or Keats. I will now give some thought to describe sunshine and me. I find it easier to work or play when the sun is shining.

On a dull day I am more prone to reading what someone else has written. Edgar Allen Poe would find some gloomy topic to put in verse on such a dreary day. Poetry is not my forte. IF I were to write a poem it would be in the hours between dark and dawn when the world is asleep. My problem being it is dark, a light would need to illuminate the scene and I would then be in another world where poetry eludes me.

I have been known to take pen and paper in hand while reclining in bed in the dark. Funny stuff to look at with the lights burning, disjointed crooked lines all swarming together. In the morning when I peruse the material, I would likely chuckle and vanity would make me save it, but hidden away where other eyes might never see it. I have done that. I would never just throw it away or alter it in any way. Sunshine conjures joy, happiness, merriment. How can one be gloomy and depressed on a bright sunny day?

* * * * * * * * *

TIME FOR CONFESSION
Lea Meadow June 2012

It was Saturday morning; my Catholic friends were headed for *CONFESSION*, for what purpose I could not fathom, at the tender age of eight, what was to confess? They ate a cookie when not allowed? Who knows, but away they went. Might as well join them; see what it's all about. Wow, what a big place the cathedral was, nothing like our modest Congregational church in the village! Must take a lot of confessions to pay for such a structure. Oh, well, not my worry. I'll just sit, mind my own business, shouldn't take too long.

Maybe my friends have lots to confess, seems like they have been gone forever. So I picked up the hymnal, and proceeded to look at the songs they sing. What's this? No notes, just words and lots of "amens". We only say amen when the prayer ends. Guess all these words are prayers, not songs! Wonder if they ever sing? How boring. Guess I will find out what happens if I confess my sins. So I enter one of those stalls with a curtain that closes out any listening in by someone sitting outside. Inside this booth is another curtain. A voice whispers "what sins did you commit since last week?" How should I know, and why does this voice think I committed any sin in the first place.

"Well, sir, mother told me not to eat any cookies before supper, so I had one, is that a sin, sir?"

"First, I am not a sir, but a father," he replied. "Did you feel any remorse when you took that cookie?" Now, that was a really dumb question. First, I don't know what remorse meant, so I guess the only thing I felt was another hunger pang, I took another cookie. How many confessions do you think that constitutes? Finding this interrogation was getting me nowhere, I left the booth, grabbed one of those skinny little cookies on the table (I guess they call that an altar) and skipped joyfully home, where I had another cookie.

* * * * * * * * *

FUN IN THE MAKING
Lea Meadow July 2012

"What shall we do?" she sighed as another long summer day loomed ahead. "We played paper dolls yesterday and with our dolls the day before, that's pretty boring." Joanne sighed back and shrugged her scrawny shoulders. Her asthma was really getting her down. I could tell whatever our activity, it would be slow and probably indoors. The kitchen drew us toward it. Out came the bread, peanut butter and jelly. It wasn't lunchtime or any other food consuming hour, but what better to do? The snacks prepared, we sat down to devour the fruits of our labors."Got it!" I shouted with glee. "How about finding Peggy and Muriel and tying them up, like cowboys and Indians. Only this time, we tie them up, not like last time. So off we trotted to find our unsuspecting victims.

We knew they would be thrilled to play with

us older girls, so enticing them to come with us was no problem. We explained the mission. We, Joanne and I, were bad strangers just come to town and we must tie them up so we could rob the bank. Sounded like fun to the unsuspecting twosome. We found two little saplings and some strong rope and got those girls out of our way.

Giggling, we retrieved our lunches and headed down the road to the old abandoned stone quarry for some alone time. Lunch over, we headed home. No little girls hanging their heads in sorrow, just two rather upset mothers ready to tie us to a tree. Spankings behind us, little girls happy to see our just reward, and we were ready to plot the next episode of revenge.

* * * * * * * * *

THE WELCOME
Lea Meadow July 2012

In the company of my Mother, we arrived at my new home, 1900 S. 4th Avenue when I was a week old. My sister was eleven years old and treated me like a very special doll. She would push me up the street to visit with her girl friends. They all took turns pushing me up and down the sidewalks. I was the ONLY living doll on the block. I wonder how many times I was removed from that carriage and slung over one shoulder or another, being passed back and forth!

Years would pass, and I was welcomed to Kindergarten and throughout the eight years of elementary school, not always with admiration. My fourth grade teacher must have thought me to be extremely unmanageable as she would admonish me: "why can't you be like your sister, Virginia", who must have been an example of blessed behavior. I never thought I was unruly, but who was I to judge! My little sister has always contended that not only was she compared to me, but to older sister, Virginia.

Sister Virginia was also an accomplished writer and worked as a correspondent for the Associated Press. Tagging along, I joined the AP, but as a copy girl, or as in today's vernacular, a "gofer". The newspaper was moving to new quarters, our AP bureau would also move ... across the street. Many printing machines, teletype lines, etc. were mule hauled across the street that spring, and we got settled in.

I met my first husband at the Associated Press, a younger man fresh out of college, who said he married me because my mother was unavailable. Not such a flattering welcome, but mother was happy. I was 25 and she thought she would be my guardian for life.

I was not an easy daughter by then, as I had been away to college, then moved out of state for several years, and my independence was dear to me. Suddenly I was being admonished for staying out too late, running with the "wrong" crowd and causing her grief. But we overcame and became good friends later.

We are welcomed into many situations throughout the years. I was welcomed into my chosen sorority, *Pi Beta Phi,* by the senior girls especially. Mother had made me an outstanding reversible coat, corduroy on one side, plaid flannel on the reverse. Both were adorned with deep pockets. Although I was "underage" I went to all the local establishments with a bottle of the forbidden tucked in a deep pocket, which became my nickname. Did I imbibe? Ah ha, you ask. You be the judge.

I later became a member of the National Society of the Daughters of the American Revolution and found myself president of the local chapter, a member of the state board and a good friend to many, many along the way. I have often felt quite welcome. I am a member of the National League of American Pen Women. This awesome group of ladies is known throughout the United States, with many very outstanding authors, painters and musicians among its members. I frequently felt undeserving of the honor of membership, for my claim to fame was editor of my high school newspaper. This qualified my credentials for membership. I continue to maintain my membership in this great group of ladies.

I joined a group of writers in Arkansas. We met once a month in a local coffee shop bookstore, where we shared our writings and self-published several editions of our endeavors. This is when I became acquainted with the fact that Ernest Hemingway had a studio/cottage in Corning, Arkansas where a group of devotees established a museum in his studio and house. Visiting this spot was an awesome experience.

When we moved to Spencer, Indiana, the local newspaper enlightened me to the existence of a new group of writers, looking to increase its membership. How great to be among another group of writers sharing their writings and insight that meets once a week. We are a group of individuals, diverse in style and deliverance. It is a joy to be a member of the group, a wonderful welcome to a new community.

My advice: just keep writing. You are all great.

* * * * * * * * *

SANTA WORE A BOW TIE
Lea Meadow July 2012

Santa comes in many sizes and shapes. But he never really seemed to fool my sons. One year a dear friend and younger by a generation, donned a Santa suit and false beard to be Santa to my off spring. Looked pretty good, well padded and ready to play his part.

So "ha, ha, ha" he descended the imaginary chimney in our old converted carriage house, and proceeded to dispatch his bag of goodies.

"Ed, who do you think you are kidding?" queried the older brother, which immediately brought forth tears of dismay from his younger brother.

If Ed hadn't been so well endowed by several pillows, his deflated ego would have been showing. Instead, he quietly proceeded to hand out the presents and "disappear" up his imaginary chimney to his equally imaginary sleigh to quickly leave the premises. Knowing Ed, I doubt that he wore a bow tie, or a tie of any description. Because the title says he did, he did.

Needless to say, Santa did not return the next year. Presents were under the tree Christmas morning that were not wrapped, and had not been under the tree the day before. Whether anyone had gone to my closet or other hiding place to see the presents before Christmas morning, I never asked and really don't care to know.

* * * * * * * * *

HOW I CONTROLLED MY LITTLE SISTER
Lea Meadow   July 2012

Does one ever really "control" another human being? Very doubtful, but we probably all try at one time or another.

My little sister was so cute it was hard to ignore her. But you certainly did NOT want to get in her face. Whether Mother, at the ripe age of 42, was just too tired to notice, Peggy had long fingernails that she learned at a very young age to use. So if you got too close, you would wear the scars of those nails.

I shared a bedroom with her. It was the smallest room in the house. She had a crib, I had a twin bed. When she got too old for the crib, she had a twin bed on the other side of the room.

There was space between the two beds, so we never actually were within touching distance. It was my duty to tell Peggy "good night" stories. Reading what someone else had written got to be boring, as she had her favorites and didn't wish to hear any others. So I began inventing stories. One I particularly enjoyed telling was of a fox who lived under my bed. I would tell her that the fox wanted to play and was about to pounce on her. The lead-up to the story became so real that it even scared me, and we would both scream and holler.

How did I learn to control my sister? I had a girl friend my age, Peg had one her age, and both girls lived across the street from us. One day my friend and I allowed Peg and her friend to play cowboys and Indians. The girls did their best to tie us to trees and then walk away. But they weren't experienced in the art of tying us up, and it was easy to escape. We were bigger and stronger and learned how to affix them to the trees enough that their mothers had to untie them. Not a good plan, and it didn't happen again.

I discovered the best way to control Peggy. There was a house being constructed in the neighborhood. Whether the builder ran out of funds or not, I am not sure. But that foundation hole stayed there for some time. The best way to deter two little pests? Get them in that hole and leave them there. It became lunchtime and no Peg showed up to eat, which concerned Mother. Finally, I had to admit that "somehow" Peg was in that hole. I'm sure Mother was only too happy to spank my behind (in those days it was ok for parents to do such a thing) and send me to somehow get that little girl out of her predicament.

Another of my favorite ways to put a stop on Peg following me to the basement involved bears. I loved to play with paper dolls, which were meticulously cut out of old Sears' catalogs. They had costumes, houses and automobiles. It was my primary play activity and messing with my elaborate layout could cause serious consequences. This was an unused area of a big rec room in the basement where my play area was undisturbed. Peg liked to "help" me and I didn't enjoy her interference. How better to stop a three year old from this activity? Invent a family of bears who would jump out and grab her if she dared to follow. So these bears gave me the privacy I felt I deserved.

Did I ever actually "control" my sister? Doubtful, at best. This all reminds me of a song from the good old days, Rosemary Clooney singing "Sisters". In going to the Internet (ah, what an invention) I discovered the song was written by none other than Irving Berlin. They just don't write songs like that anymore.

* * * * * * * * *

I SAW THE ANSWER IN THE FIRELIGHT
Lea Meadow August 2012

The question had been niggling at the back of my mind all day. Twilight came and the fireplace was lit, emitting a nice warm glow on the late autumn evening. The answer was really quite simple. But first, the question. I had gone shopping at the Mall earlier in the day, and someone had side-swiped my brand new 2012 *Camero,* a car I had dreamed of owning ever since the model appeared on the market. Why I had parked in such a vulnerable spot, no one will ever imagine. Possibly, it was in part due to the fact that I just wanted to show off.

How could I ever explain my predicament to my ever-loving spouse without sounding like a rotten, spoiled brat? What if he were to take away my driving privileges, even for one teensy day? Not that I really had any place special to go, but rather the idea that I couldn't go. Then, in the light of the magical fireplace, I saw the answer. Just don't tell him. Why would he notice it in the first place, as it was sitting with the damage to the wall of the garage? All I had to do was not mention it, and in the morning I could take it to the mechanic and get it repaired.

All day my dilemma had plagued me, and right there, in the glow of the firelight I had the solution. All that trauma for nothing.

* * * * * * * * *

UNDERSTANDING THE LOOK ON A PERSON'S FACE
Lea Meadow August 2012

When Mary smiled at me, I could never tell if she was genuinely pleased to see me or if it was a face she donned whenever she approached another human being. We had been close friends in high school, UNTIL I joined a group of five other girls in my class who seemed to have much in common with my desires to be "one of the gang".

I had always been a shy girl, afraid that I would be rejected. I was an only child, always going wherever my parents went. The first time I was invited to a classmate's birthday party, upon arrival I hid in the nearest closet. If the children were inclined to play "hide and seek", it probably wouldn't have been long before I "was found". But in my desire to get away this thought did not enter my mind.

Mary's mother had seen me slither into the closet and when refreshments were served, she opened the door to my escape and handed me a plate with cake and ice cream. Her smile warmed my heart and I followed her into the kitchen, where she kindly gave me a smile, a look of understanding. It did the trick.

Once, many years later, I was invited to a big political rally. The same stomach churning sent chills up and down my spine. These were people I had known for many years. I was looking forward to the event. Why this sudden holding back, this fear to join the crowd?

I remembered the kind look of understanding

on Mary's mother's face, how she had helped me overcome my fears. So smiling to myself, I joined the others, had a drink and all was well.

* * * * * * * * *

THE RAGING RIVER
Lea Meadow August 2012

It had rained for nearly a week solid when the skies began to lift. We lived at the top of a long hill where we were relatively safe from flooding ... relatively, but not entirely, as we had three or four ponds on our property that all went over their banks, just lower than the spot where our home stood.

The little town of Williford, Arkansas was situated at the bottom of that long hill, right in the path of the beautiful Spring River, loved by canoe and raft advocates for decades. The town was surrounded by farms, small but big enough to sustain a few head of cattle.

Fortunately for us, we had not been residents of the area during the BIG flood of 1982, which reached from the Canadian border, down the Great Mississippi and the equally ominous Missouri rivers, with the Ohio happy to add to the raging waters. But the flood that occurred later in the 1990s was bad enough to make long time residents relieved in its shorter duration.

The flood of the 1990s swamped the low-lying pasture land causing the cows to walk over the fence. We were new residents of Arkansas. Whether it was curiosity or a desire to help those less fortunate, we climbed into our car and headed down hill. On the river side of the highway that went across town stood the Post Office. We had to stop the car before we got to the parking lot, as the road was impassable.

When the flood of 1982 took out the bridge across the river, the engineers had the foresight to replace it with a much higher bridge. However, the water was right up to the side of the road that led to several cattle farms.

****

The following is a writing assignment that required the participants to write a story using ONLY three word sentences:

****

DAY IS DONE
Nancy Thurston 8/26/08

It is morning. Out of bed. I stretch, shower. Drink strong coffee. Watch says late. Grab bagel, run. Catch my ride. Work is dull. Lunch is boring. Work still dull. Cell phone rings. Evening date planned! She's a looker. Have fabulous evening. Refuses etching offer. That is OK. Take it slow. Another day dawning.

****

LIVING FOR THE PRESENT
Lea Meadow

Christmas time and childhood bring memories of the days when the den/sewing room was closed off from the prying eyes of young girls, eager to see what the seamstress was so busy doing while we were (presumably) asleep.

Mother was an accomplished seamstress. All our clothing was handmade, from underpants to outer snow apparel. She could even make dolls! There was quite an expanse of years between the three siblings. Our oldest sister was eleven when I was born, sixteen when Peg came along.

One year she made us matching felt skirts, the circular style popular in the fifties. The clothes were always nice, although homemade. My girlfriends all had store-bought outfits, which I thought were awesome. So when I was sixteen and old enough to find employment, I bought a corduroy skirt.

The Christmas she made the rag dolls was the ultimate. If my extreme need to peek hadn't been prevalent, it would have been more of a surprise to find the dolls under the Christmas tree on Christmas morning. I'm sure Mother knew I had peeked, but I tried to act very surprised. The doll has held up well all these years later.

That was one kind of present. The year we gave Pierce his very own shotgun was a surprise of an entirely different nature. My father had the gun hidden in the trunk of his Studebaker. The two of us had decided to prolong the giving of the gift. Daddy came through the door of our humble apartment carrying a long, skinny box. Pierce tore into the package with haste. How great was his amazement when he found himself staring at the handle of a broom! NEVER play practical jokes on an Irishman, not that Irishman, for sure. The box, the broom and many foul words were flung across that small living space. When the temper settled down to a small flare, the box holding the real shotgun was presented.

Such are the examples this writer sets forth for the title, "Living for the Present."

* * * * * * * * *

PRAISE FOR THE P
Lea Meadow October 2012

Hallelujah! Let's praise the **P**. The what, or is it the who or the why? First, **P** is the sixteenth letter in our alphabet. Who put it there, and why? Not for me to say. But we shall now praise the **P**.

Purple begins with the letter **P**, and purple is my favorite color, so Praise, ye, oh wonderful **P**! Patience begins with **P**. Patience is a virtue, or so it says somewhere in my archives of phrases learned.

Patience is not one of my stronger traits, so we will stop there.

Who decided **P** should find a spot in our alphabet? Do Native Americans have a **P** in their alphabet? Or the highlanders of Tibet? Don't know, don't really care. I just need to deal with the **P** in the title of this rather nonsensical topic that I drew out of the basket for today's assignment.

Polite begins with a **P**, so please be polite as

you labor through this ordeal. Thank you. People begin with a **P**. Now we know all sorts of people, some who certainly are not polite, or patient, never look good in purple but when upset their skin takes on a purple hue. Stay away from those individuals for you never know what may hit you.

Perseverance is a long word that I needed to peruse the dictionary for the proper spelling. I got to "peruse" to find that. I peruse lots of books for enjoyment, but reading the dictionary is not one of my most favorite pastimes. That presumes I know how to spell!

We could get technical or see how many words in this piece begin with the letter **P**, but it would be more entertaining to find out what some other would-be author drew out of that basket to enlighten us today.

* * * * * * * * *

A MEMORABLE FAMILY REUNION
Lea Meadow

Family reunions were a way of life growing up. It was an annual affair, falling on Grandma's birthday, September 1, every year she was alive . . . and she lived for ninety years. After that, the date was set for *Father's Day* in June. After I left home in 1960, attendance for me was nil until venturing to the final attempt in 1990, which was a bad weather event to leave for another time.

When I married the first time and moved to New England, family took on a whole new meaning . . . my husband and my children, with occasional visits from grandparents and our annual trip "home" to visit my folks, my sister and the nieces and nephew. When my parents died in the mid 1970's, even those visits ceased.

In 2005 I regretted that the clan was no longer gathering, and one long winter's night in January, I hatched an idea which culminated in *THE PLAN*. We needed to gather one more time for a *Cousin Reunion*.

There had been 25 of us cousins growing up, with an age span of several decades.

Sadly, by 2005 only twelve of us remained amongst the living. My sister, the youngest cousin, was very skeptical of my hair-brained idea, said no one would respond, and she didn't want any part of it. But, my stubbornness prevailed, letters were sent and replies received. General consensus, go for it!

To make the event a real success, I decided it was only fitting to also invite all the spouses and all the surviving widows of those thirteen cousins who hopefully would be watching us from above. Maybe even wish they could join us, just one more time!

The date was set for, no less, Father's Day weekend. Only one cousin would not to be able to attend, as he was in a hospital and not doing well. Two widows were also indisposed and one living spouse, my very own brother-in-law, stayed home. We met in the Senior Center of our tiny little "hometown" in southwestern Minnesota, filling the meeting room with twenty-five boisterous relatives in attendance.

My husband and I arrived early and set out the *big* "Voss Reunion" sign, which we had made especially for the occasion, on the front yard. There was no mistaking that our clan was about to meet.

As the guests arrived, the name tags which I had made for each participant were donned. Each cousin and widow was presented with a manila folder that held genealogical sheets which I had complied on the computer, using information that I had requested prior to the big day. Family reunions are NOTHING without food, and the tables groaned under the weight of all those homemade goodies.

Family recipe books were also a tradition in our clan, recipes well worth sharing. We settled down for some serious reminiscing, with coffee and sweet rolls to sustain us until lunch. Everyone brought scrapbooks, photo albums and family memorabilia. We set up several tables to hold these items and gathered around the room to get reacquainted. We are all getting older, hearing and eyesight beginning to fade, so the room was noisy, to say the least. Also, our family, all sons and daughters of our grandmother's children, tended to be boisterous even in youth . . . laughter being a big part of life. Practical jokes included. We also tend to exaggerate, so retelling of stories grow with the telling. There is always some family member to set it straight by telling their version.

Most of the family live within a hundred mile radius of each other, with the exception of three of us, one in Chicago, one in Orlando and *moi* in Arkansas. I was definitely the *outsider*, and my husband was a stranger to all but my sister. But we two served as hosts and carried the day without serious hitches. The round tables were set close together, but not too close, so that all could participate in conversations around the room. Cameras were flashing all day, candid and posed.

After all those absent years, I was pleased to recognize my cousins and call them by the right name. The widows of cousins were a little tricky for me, as some of them I had never met. The process of elimination helped in the identification process. It was pleasant watching the various individuals looking at the pictures and reading books, laughing and taking something of interest to show and share with someone else.

Our family ties are founded in the Schleswig-Holstein region of Germany. One cousin brought a huge old map of that area, which I later had restored and hangs in my den. The towns from which our ancestors migrated were all marked, which was very helpful.

We had a story telling hour before lunch, in which exaggerated tales of youthful adventures were shared. Tears and laughter resounded across the room. There were letters from relatives in Germany that were written in the 1950s. They had been written in German and my son, who married a German girl while stationed in Germany translated them for us. One cousin read them aloud to the group. They were filled with insights into life in post World War II Germany . . . very poignant.

Just before we broke for lunch I decided to say a "few words." I wanted to thank everyone for being there . . . and it was just a few words, as I started to choke up and cried . . . guess everyone got the point. Grace was said, plates were filled and the feast begun. The afternoon was spent looking through all the memorabilia, pictures, study of the map and good old fashioned talk. Although we had all eaten more than necessary at noon, a catered meal ended this magnificent day.

Festivities did not cease at the close of day. My husband and I stayed in the area that night and went door to door the next day for more intimate moments with each cousin and spouse living in the area. We ate strawberries fresh from the garden, sweet and juicy, while looking at additional pictures. Rhubarb is a favorite fruit of mine, one sorely missed in Arkansas where it is too hot to grow. Several relatives were able to satisfy some of those cravings with pie, cookies and rhubarb/strawberry sauce! Yum!

We try to keep in touch with Christmas cards, e-mails and telephone calls. It is not easy, as we had drifted far afield over the years. I have made it a mission to send *everyone* a Christmas letter which includes some tidbits from our common past. It is hoped that this jolt on my part is well received. With some I shall never know.

A family is forever, no matter how we drift apart. The members are not to be taken lightly. I am forever grateful for this hair-brained idea, and cherish the memories, the love and the people who comprise my family, my world.

* * * * * * * * *

LOVE IS WARM
Lea Meadow 11/9/12

Love of a husband and wife is warm. The love a mother has for her newborn child is warm. Love that keeps you warm may come in many forms.

The new husband looks at his bride with loving awe . . . "how blessed am I to have found such a wonderful woman!" he marvels. She is equally awestruck, and wonders secretly how long this bliss will last.

The arrival of the first-born child fills them

both with love and admiration. The baby nestled in the mother's arms is so warm and trusting! How sweet it is! The colic that dominates their lives for those first few months is tempered by that love, and a routine is established where love flourishes.

There is the warmth of the fireplace on a cold winter's evening. You snuggle close together on the sofa, a warm cup of hot chocolate to take the edge off the bitter cold outside. His love for you keeps your heart warm, the cocoa warms your inner self and all is right with the world.

An individual loves in many ways. The joy of watching the winter birds at feed outside your window warms you with contentment. They bustle about, eating the morsels that you have thoughtfully provided. You see the snow glistening on the ground and spy the two deer crossing the field, stopping to devour the corn that you trudged through the snow to set about for their enjoyment and nourishment, you are warmed by the sight.

The postman arrives with a package from loved ones. The warmth felt by their kindness in remembering the date, be it an anniversary or a thank you, makes you realize that you are appreciated.

Night comes and the bed is chilly from the long hours of idleness waiting for your arrival. He reaches across the small chasm that separates you, puts his arms around you and whispers, "I love you", and you warm from his embrace, his kind words.

Love is sweet, love is warm.

* * * * * * * * *

MY BEST HABIT
Lea Meadow

We have bad habits. We have good habits. My best habit must fall under the category of "good."

I have practiced this habit for enough years that I have lost count. It began when I was having trouble with the circulation in my legs, that I recollect. So, every morning, before I arise for the day, I go through my exercises. They are not exhausting and do not require the need to actually "get out of bed."

The first set is done flat on my back. I stretch my arms above my head, actually using the headboard for leverage. Then I do leg exercises, bringing my lower legs up, stretching, etc. There are several exercises in this set.

Now it is time to sit up with my legs hanging over the side of the bed. I twist my neck left and right, up and down. Then I exercise the right arm, bringing it directly up in the air, repeat with the left arm. Then the right arm swings out to the right, then the left and repeat with the left arm.

Time to exercise the legs. Still sitting on the edge of the bed, I bring both legs straight out in front of me, then angle the feet so the toes are up, then down. With legs bent, I twist ankles to the right, then left. Finally, it is time to do one leg at a time. First the right leg, which has been dangling straight down, with knee still bent goes upward toward the ceiling, repeat five to ten times, then do the left leg.

All of these gyrations take about twenty

minutes. Time to slip into my robe and slippers and trudge out to the kitchen for my cup-a-joe, black, please, and truly greet the day.

* * * * * * * * *

OH, NO, ANOTHER RED LIGHT
Lea Meadow 12/7/12

I was cruising along the Long Island Expressway, on my way home from shopping at the local stores, mindful of my day ahead, when sirens blew, lights flashed and I dutifully pulled over to the side of the road.

The officer promptly departed his vehicle, ticket pad and pen in hand. I rolled down my window and asked if there was a problem. He abruptly informed me that I had run a red light, to which I replied that the light had been orange when I began crossing the intersection, which I assumed meant that I could proceed with caution.

Not too nicely, he demanded that I get out of the car and show him this orange light. I described that the orange light was placed in the middle between red and green.

What to my amazement when I discovered that in New York City and suburbs, there is NO orange light! He just shook his head, suggested that I take a written and oral driver's test ASAP, update my South Dakota license to New York and try to behave.

He made sure I would do this by closely following me to the nearest DMV.

Not too many years later we moved over the state border into Massachusetts, where I continued to disobey the laws of the road. It was a cold, bleak January morning. My New York plates had expired, which I purposely did not renew as I was moving to Massachusetts. While still in New York State, I was pulled over by another irate officer.

How he ascertained that my plates had expired, I still ponder, as they were so mud impacted he must have had x-ray vision to read the numbers, let alone the date.

My oldest child was eight at the time, the

youngest three. My five year old middle child and the three year old both began to cry, pleading with the officer not to arrest their mother. The officer promptly issued me a warning to see that the matter was solved pronto, and we went on our way to our new home (a converted carriage house, cold as cold could be . . . another story there.) As soon as possible, I marched to the local DMV office, got Massachusetts plates and license, and sighed in relief that I could now concentrate on settling in to country life on the outskirts of a little Massachusetts village.

    Several years later I went to work at the local Massachusetts DMV as a clerk. In doing a background check on their new employee, it was discovered that I had been in trouble with the New York DMV, and also the officer, Mr. Zucco, who worked out of the office in which I was now employed. Much laughter ensued upon learning the history of their latest employee. It was a fun job.

* *

ONCE A DAY, EVERY DAY
Lea Meadow

Habits, especially those deemed positive, can be very helpful. For as many years as I can remember, I have started my day with exercises. Nothing strenuous, but helpful in getting the kinks out, stretching those limbs kind of exercises.

Therefore, every morning before my feet hit the floor, I stretch my arms above my head, then take those lower extremities from beneath the blankets and stretch those feet and lower legs.

Now it is time to sit up, dangle my legs over the edge of the bed and first work on those arms. Up above my head, then right and then left. Now, one arm at a time: right, left and up. Repeat five times.

Now for the legs: both straight out in front of me, then beginning with the right leg, move that ankle to the right, flex and wiggle: repeat with the left leg. Time to turn those ankles: right ankle rotate from right to left: repeat five times. Then do the same with the left leg. Now bring the right knee up high, lower it, repeat five times. Time to stretch the left knee (ooh, crack!) and repeat that exercise with the right leg.

Finally, it is time to slip into my slippers and trot out to the kitchen for the real eye-opener: my first cup of coffee. THEN, when that has been consumed, return to the bedroom, anticipate the clothing needed, wash my face and get dressed.

The day may now proceed.

* * * * * * * * *

I WALKED INTO QUICKSAND
Lea Meadow 12/21/12

When you open your mouth, you frequently "walk into quicksand". In other words, your feet sink deep in the rut you have made, the rest of the body follows quickly in step, and you are well on your way.

When I married for the second time, we both brought children from our previous dalliances with unsuccessful marriages. My oldest, a daughter, was away at school, my two sons were still at home, one in elementary, the other in junior high. His five children were living with their aunt and uncle and quite happy where they were.

However, we decided it was time that the two families became one, were living in a big old farm house with lots of land, and joined forces. That was probably a dream, with nothing to do with reality, as we soon discovered.

Sibling rivalry prevailed. Both "Mom" and "Dad" were busy working and the proverbial fan hit it hard. His two youngest children, both girls, decided a step-mother was nothing they wished to have, and moved back with their aunt and uncle. We visited a couple of times, the welcome mat remained out of sight, and we took tail back home.

That definitely spells quicksand in my book.

There is another kind of quicksand, the kind found at some beaches. You may be joyfully traipsing along, and suddenly you get this sinking sensation.

You look down to discover your feet are no longer in sight, you then high step it out of danger's way and "get out of Dodge."

The third kind of quicksand I have personally encountered happened when I served as one of three Selectmen in our small community in Massachusetts. It is quite easy to upset members of the community when you "officially" clamp down on someone's activities! Ooh, my, the repercussions that can occur! I was not reelected to that board, but couldn't keep out of politics, so I joined the local Board of Zoning Appeals. Oops, not a good move. When we left Massachusetts very early in the morning, it was with the sheriff on our heels to serve me, as a member of that board, with a summons to appear in court. We lived just a few miles from the New York State border, left our happy home and literally flew into the next state before we took a deep breath. Not funny at the time, but in retrospect, good for a number of good laughs.

My most embarrassing moment came shortly before that second marriage. My divorce papers were still wet. His had been contested. We hurried east to face our day in court, where the proper papers appeared. Memory says that somewhere in that court proceeding, my big mouth flapped a little too loudly, and the judge admonished me with the remark that I was "only a luxury".

In conclusion I can honestly say that I have walked in quicksand. With my nature it could happen again and again. Keeps the calluses at bay.

* * * * * * * * *

GROWING UP MIDDAUGH
Lea Meadow   8/24/10

(This is a brief excerpt from the book that Lea Meadow is writing about her family history.)

In order to bring semblance to our family history during the early years in the life of Edna Middaugh, and due to the lack of written family documentation of those years from 1869 to the end of the nineteenth century, a diversion is necessary. Therefore, I have taken the liberty to use information found in Volume I of *History of*

Jackson County, an illustrated history of Jackson County, Minnesota, by Arthur P. Rose, and published in 1910. The following will be interspersed with family lore and Rose's book:

Growing up in rural southwest Minnesota in 1874 would have been a challenge that those of us today can hardly imagine, let alone tolerate. There were no indoor bathrooms, or other plumbing, no electricity, no telephones or automobiles. The learning process was either at home or at the home of a "teacher."

Crops were cultivated by hand, from preparing the soil to planting the seeds to harvesting the crop. There were no irrigation ditches or fancy automatic watering devises for the fields. Man relied on Nature and God for his survival. Edna's two older brothers, Elmer Eugene and Richard Adelbert, spent their days in those fields with their father, grandfather and various uncles who were their neighbors.

Edna would have learned at a very young age to help with the domestic side of the household. There are no pictures that show us the structure of the homes they inhabited. Were they sod or log? We may never know. What we do know is that our ancestors were pioneers of the soil, and they migrated many times.

Edna would be ten years old before her little sister, Orra Amelia Katherine, was born. Both of their parents would have been forty-three years old, weary from the daily trials of their lifestyle.

Petersburg was a small farming township in Jackson County, Minnesota. There were relatives, including her maternal grandfather and step-grandmother, an assortment of aunts, uncles and cousins living nearby. Grandfather Gruhlke farmed the land adjacent to the Middaugh land. The children had an adoring grandmother, *Grossmuter* Gruhlke. She was tiny, but tough. She had raised her four stepchildren and seven of her own, having much experience in the rearing of *der kinder*. German was the preferred tongue in the Gruhlke household. But, Solomon, Adeline and the four children would have also spoken English.

The population in Jackson County increased sufficiently in 1869, the year that the Gruhlkes and Solomon Middaugh moved there from Waseca County, Minnesota. According to the *History of Jackson County, Vol. I,* "There was a large increase in population, many of the new settlers penetrating to theretofore unsettled portions of the county. It became known that the country would produce bountiful crops of wheat, and the prairies became dotted with the sod shanties and dugouts of the new settlers."

    Petersburg Township had a population of 244 in 1869, with 83 acres cultivated. The *History of Jackson County* recorded the winter of 1869-1870 was exceptionally severe, lingering into spring. Severest blizzards occurred in March between the fifteenth and sixteenth. Roads became impassible and many houses drifted over with snow. Shops closed and people stayed home. The following week, history repeated itself with another blizzard.

    These were the conditions that faced the pioneering peoples of that era. During the spring of 1870, "many who had come the previous year and filed on claims and then gone away for the winter came back to take possession of their land," making improvements and beginning their farming endeavors. Land records on file indicate August Gruhlke filed his land in 1872. In 1874, Solomon Middaugh filed his claim for 160 acres in the same quadrant as his father-in-law, August, and brother-in-law, Edward Gruhlke. Edward was the youngest brother of Adeline Gruhlke Middaugh, my great-grandmother. All these acres were located in Petersburg Township. The three men were in Petersburg according to the 1870 United States census.

What was the mode of transportation for these hardy folk? There were horses and carriages, and the romanticized "prairie schooner" or covered wagon. As the Gruhlkes and Solomon Middaugh migrated from Waseca County to Jackson County, from established households, we at least may pretend that they traveled by schooner. As a child, I used to fantasize about crossing the country in a covered wagon, never realizing that my great-grandparents probably had done just that! I always liked to think that I had lived in another time, some ancestor from the past, guiding my dreams!

Rose wrote, "Agriculture was not the principal industry of the late 1860's and early 1870's." It was difficult to get base products, such as grain, to mills that could grind grain into flour. So these early settlers concentrated primarily on maintaining a quality life for their families. They raised vegetables and grain for their own use and occupied their time in other pursuits of income. They were blacksmiths, tanners, coopers, teachers and lay clergymen. They were also trappers. Wild animals were in great abundance, especially small fur-bearing animals, such as mink, foxes and badgers, the hides from which were in demand back East.

By 1869, when the Gruhlkes and Solomon Middaugh came to Jackson County, the prairies were "dotted with the sod shanties and dugouts of the new settlers." This indicated that building a sound structure in which to live was low on the list of priorities. The primary concern would have been in clearing the land to make it arable for the planting of crops.

When these pioneers returned in the spring of 1870, in addition to bringing their families, they brought cattle, horses, sheep, hogs and farming implements such as hoes, rakes, machetes and shovels, all tools used to prepare the sowing of seeds. The spring of 1870 was ideal and "a fair crop of wheat and other grain was raised." Rose stated that in July a drought reduced the crops of corn and wheat, but did not wipe them out.

Records indicate that all four Middaugh children were born in Jackson County. However, Elmer Eugene Middaugh was born in October 1869 so was possibly born in Waseca County, where the families had previously lived. Richard was born in 1872, followed by Edna in 1874 and Orra in 1884, all in Jackson County.

Solomon Middaugh was the only member of his immediate family who migrated from Waseca and Steele Counties to Jackson County. Adeline's father, August, and his wife, Wilhelmina, came with enumerable sons and a daughter, Ida. Also living in Jackson County were Edward and Sophia Gruhlke.

* * * * * * * * *

INN KEEPING
Lea Meadow

My name is Ethan Smythe. My family came to North America in 1668 and settled in the western part of Massachusetts, one of the first colonies established in the New World.

It was important that we have a trade that would provide us with the ability to barter for goods from other settlers in our area. The population at the time was sparse, but travel into the middle of the new country was growing on a daily basis. There was much talk of less populated country to be found in the west, with large valleys that could sustain farms that would produce the much-needed food for the travelers and settlers to the new land.

Father came from a long line of English merchants and was well versed in the necessary stock that would enable travelers along the way. He built a small General Store next to the Inn, where he kept a good supply of the staples these travelers would need. There was a stable for the horses that pulled the wagons and a small area where the stagecoaches could park while the drivers and passengers partook of a good, solid New England meal and found comfortable beds to rest their weary bones before continuing the road west.

This road was to be called the "Boston Post" Road, for there were a number of riders and coaches that carried the long-awaited mail to the new comers to America. Father always bragged that Paul Revere slept there, but history has never proved this fact one way or another. It makes a good tale to tell while huddled in front of the blazing fire, drinking ale and telling of the many adventures met along the way.

The old inn in which you just spent the night was a popular stopping place on the Boston Post Road that traversed between New York City and Boston. It is therefore a possibility that the Inn here in Hudson, Massachusetts was visited by prominent men of the day. If the walls could talk, the tales they could tell!

* * * * * * * * *

TELL IT TO THE WIND
Lea Meadow

I sit here in my adobe hut on the prairies of the new territory known as Minnesota and wish to howl like the wind that persistently blows outside these thin, but sturdy walls. I contemplate why we ever left our lovely home in western Massachusetts to traverse to this God-forsaken expanse of tumbleweed and wind.

Women follow their men, and this is where we have stopped. Our first weeks were spent within the Conestoga wagons that brought us – men, women and children – here to find a better place to raise our children and our crops, which will sustain us through the cold months. It is cold. The wind continually blows. Its constant battering brings tears to my eyes and I sob uncontrollably, longing for the life we left behind. I can only pray that the good Lord above is watching over us and will keep us from harm's way.

We have heard of the Indian massacres just over the ridge in northern Iowa, fervently hoping that they are satisfied where they are and do not venture into this terrain. We have never encountered these savages, but understand from neighbors who have been longer that they are more brutal than those beasts we had among us in Massachusetts.

We lost several members of our party when we crossed Indiana and Illinois. Many succumbed to illness and malnutrition. Others literally went crazy crossing the unending flat prairies and were left to parish by themselves. We regret that we were unable to assist them in their hours of grief. We were unable to bury them along the way, and were forced to carry their wooden coffins in a wagon. Upon arriving here in southern Minnesota, we have been fortunate in obtaining land for a cemetery, which sits high on a hill overlooking the valley and Des Moines River below us, may their souls find peace.

* * * * * * * * *

LOOKING FOR A HOME
Lea Meadow

Although I never expect to look for another home, there are structures I wouldn't mind dwelling within. One of them is a Tudor Manor style home, something I have always found interesting, ever since I was a child.

Traveling to elementary school, a short mile from home, I would pass by such a house, wondering if one needed to be wealthy to live in such splendor. The owners were wealthy jewelers and had no children I could visit, so I never did get inside.

I grew up in a large two story colonial, so was used to lots of space in which to roam. When I first married, an apartment was all we could afford, furnished with hand-me-down furniture and little space to traverse. So I continued to dream of the day I could live in a big home of my own.

The second time I married, while living in Massachusetts, we decided that "taxachusetts" was becoming beyond our means of survival. I literally put my finger on a map of the United States, and ended up living in a small Ozark community in Arkansas, where we operated a General Store for five years. Tiring of this occupation, we purchased twenty acres down the road and lived in a very small one-bedroom house with a very leaky basement recreation room where we spent most of our at-home hours. THEN we came into an inheritance and built a new home on the other side of the drive way that was very, very large.

Because we both have family living north of Arkansas, mine residing in South Dakota and my husband's in Massachusetts, Spencer, Indiana looked to be about mid-way between the two areas. So, here we are, here we will stay and no longer must we look for a home. This is it.

* * * * * * * * *

A DRIVE IN THE COUNTRY
Lea Meadow

I learned to drive the old 1939 Studebaker one Sunday when I rode with Daddy out in the country to get farm-fresh eggs, a treat that we always enjoyed. Suddenly, Daddy stopped the car, told me to get out and we switched positions. I was behind the wheel, just old enough to see over the steering wheel and touch the floor pedals. Daddy showed me the different locations of the stick that would get me in the right gear. After a few attempts to get the feel of putting the left foot on the proper place and being shown where the different gears were located, and what function they served, we off to a jolting start.

All went well for a mile or so, when suddenly, right in there, in the middle of the road ahead, stood a big old cow. "Daddy, what shall I do?" I nervously inquired. "Stop the car. The cow will move on all by herself." What a revelation! The cow moved and we proceeded to the city limits, where I turned over the operation of the motor vehicle to my father, and we safely arrived back home, no cracked eggs, no severely damaged ego.

* * * * * * * * *

THE BIRDS FLEW SOUTH
Lea Meadow 2/8/13

The Story of the Little Robin Walking to Missouri

I was late leaving my summer home in South Dakota. My kin had already begun the long flight south for the winter. I had a broken wing that wouldn't heal, so flight was out of the question for me.

Thus began my long, arduous journey by foot. I had to stock up on food that would sustain me as I set off. Fortunately, the lady that lived in the house next to the tree where I had a nest daily filled her bird feeders with an ample supply of seeds and nuts, which would supplement the meager cache of worms who had not dug very deep holes in her well irrigated back yard. My feathered friends had pretty much cleared out that worm supply before they flew south.

I began my long walk south. How different it is for a bird that usually flies to find itself walking, walking and walking some more. There were tall, prickly weeds in the fields surrounding her meticulous yard which bit into my tender toes and scraped my under feathers, sticking my tender skin beneath my feathers. Mother never told me about a callous or bunions and such.

Birds fly south because they have wings. They don't walk to Missouri, unless you are that poor little robin walking to Missouri, as some human wrote about in a song. It didn't take me long to have that "Tear drop in my eye!"

I could write volumes about the things a bird might see if it walked from South Dakota to Missouri. There were fields and streams to cross, not to mention roads where cars sped by without so much as a sideways glance in my direction. I couldn't fly from their oncoming approach, just quickly hop out of the way. The fields seemed endlessly long, filled with holes and ruts made by the big tractors the farmers use to plow those fields. Fortunately, the farmer cannot gather up all the seeds left from the hay he cuts, so I have good ground food to eat on my journey.

The streams presented a greater problem. Birds fly over streams and other bodies of water, but if you can't fly, how do you cross that water. I tried to walk along the right bank to find a spot to cross to the left bank. By the time I found a good spot, I had walked miles out of my direct path to Missouri and there I was, in Nebraska. Figured I might as well see the big city while I was there. After that adventure, I decided to leave city living in Omaha to the humans. Too much traffic and noise.

Finally I have left that clamor behind me. By walking along the side of the roads mankind has so thoughtfully built, keeping well away from the exhaust of all those vehicles, I am on my way south, where it is purported that the days don't get so cold in the winter as they do in South Dakota.

Next time you pass a poor little robin walking

to Missouri, stop and give him a ride. He will be sure to pass along the word to his kin that they feather their nests with special care while sitting in your tree.

* * * * * * * * *

CHILDHOOD MYTHS AND OTHER THINGS
Lea Meadow 2/15/13

My little sister is five years my junior. As children, we shared a bedroom with twin beds, with a rug that separated us. It was a small room. Mother delegated me with the responsibility of reading a bedtime story to this adorable little girl.

"Uncle Wiggly" was her favorite. I was tired of Uncle Wiggly and Nurse Jane Fuzzy Wuzzy. I knew those stories by heart from the many times of telling them. Thus, it was time to invent some stories of my own.

I convinced my sister, Peg, that there were foxes living under the bed and if she were to put her feet on the floor they would reach out and grab her. Thus she would remain in her bed and I did not need to worry that she would attempt to climb into bed with me.

We had a lovely big basement, with a large recreation room. At one end Mother had set up her sewing machine where she assembled all our clothing, from underwear to outerwear. At the other end of the room, we girls had set up a permanent collection of paper dolls, carefully cut out from *Sears and Roebuck* catalogs, complete with changes of clothing and every type of furniture found within the catalogs. We could entertain ourselves for hours on end.

Of course, to reach this haven, it was necessary to descend the steps that led to that region. These steps had no back, just boards attached to side railings, etc. In order to hamper little sister from trailing me to this wonderful hide-a-way, I convinced her there was a family of bears under those stairs. One needed to move rapidly in order not to get caught.

Regarding another thing: have you ever wondered what is kept in those metal structures that dotted the farmer's fields? As a child, my curiosity was tremendous. There was writing on those storage units that I *thought* said "butter". On a hot summer day, how did the farmer keep the butter from melting? What to my amazement when one day I read it correctly – Butler!

And finally, we can't forget Shirley, who appears in several places in the Bible. You may recall her – Shirley the cross-eyed bear? Or, Shirley goodness and mercy shall follow me, etc. I always figured she was quite a personality to find such prominence to be placed in the Bible.

Childhood is a wonderful time. Imagination is what makes us good writers. The pair can't be beat.

* * * * * * * * *

WHEN ROADS BECAME SLIPPERY
Lea Meadow 2/22/13

It was December 26, 2000 and we were stranded at home as a very serious ice storm hit northern Arkansas, leaving many people without power. No electricity, no heat, no telephone service, even the cell towers were down, nothing at all to connect you with the outside world. And you certainly did NOT wish to venture outside at all. There was ice everywhere. It was dark. It was cold. There were not enough clothes in the closet and drawers to keep that cold from penetrating your body.

Understand, if you have no power, there is not any warm coffee from coffee makers to take the chill off those bones. However, we had a gas cook top where we could make coffee with an old coffee pot we had kept. Yet there is absolutely nothing you can do to warm up. So you huddle and you pray that power will be restored very, very soon.

It did not happen. We had two fireplaces.

One was in the Great Room with its 16 foot ceiling. Heat rises, way up. It took us a day or more to realize that in the basement the ceiling was only seven feet from the floor and there was a fireplace there. Big deal. A gas fireplace may do some good, but you remain somewhat cold. This misadventure lasted and lasted. By day eight one felt so grimy and uncomfortable you remain past caring.

We had two full sized freezers that were both filled to capacity. There was nothing to do except hope that power would be restored before everything thawed and would need to be thrown out. Needless to say, it finally came to the realization that food would not keep, so it got tossed out. Innumerable vultures descended on our field, relishing in our loss. They made quick work of eating our loss.

It is sad to say, but true. When day nine arrived and the power was restored one felt an air of disappointment. We had survived and felt confident that we could continue to survive, but now we were inundated with light and heat. We had a well that remained frozen long enough that we traveled the 20 miles to the nearest Wal Mart for some bottled water . . . not little bottles, but big, gallon jugs. There were toilets to flush, faces to wash and teeth to brush. Dirty clothes could continue to pile up, but the bare necessities just couldn't continue not to exist.

There is much to be said about greed. Water and lamp oil were being grabbed from the hands of the clerks in Wal Mart when the many pallets of the precious water arrived. The clerks finally gave up and left the hoards to grab water straight from the pallets. The men just got out of the way as quickly as they could.

The trip to the store was awesome. Our gravel driveway was over 300 feet long, and covered with a thick layer of ice. The roads had some sand covering the slippery pavement, but the ruts were deep and travel was risky at best.

This was Arkansas, a border state between North and South. You don't have to reside in Massachusetts or Indiana to feel the ravage of Old Man Winter. Mother Nature will have her way.

* * * * * * * * *

WHY DO WE PROCRASTINATE?
Lea Meadow 2/25/13

I must get busy and write as I have to leave home to arrive at the Guild for our regular Friday afternoon meeting of the Writer's Group.

Once I get started with the writing, I won't have any problem finishing the assignment. It's the getting started that always has me stumped.

Why procrastinate? I spent a good number of the early morning hours, delaying my return to slumber land, day dreaming of what I would write. Now I sit here before my computer, at a loss for words that will describe my need to procrastinate.

What if I were to fail in this assignment? What if no one likes what I write? Will they be too polite to criticize, or will they snicker at my feeble attempt? Why do I care?

Oh, good, time for a snack break. I am too hungry to write at this time. Maybe later the mood will be upon me to write something meaningful that my fellow writers will appreciate.

Or, maybe they will go home and tell the world about this dumb woman who thinks she can write. Whatever, let them, I don't care.

Why procrastinate? For some, it could be the simple reason that if the task is completed it will be time to do some other menial job that we have been putting off for a rainy day. It could be that we are afraid of rejection.

Maybe we just don't have the confidence in ourselves to "do something" . . . for the fear of failure. If you don't attempt to perform a task, how can you fail? No one will be the wiser.

Must be lunch time. Good. I don't have to worry about why I procrastinate. Until later.

* * * * * * * * *

A QUIET DREAM
Lea Meadow

I awoke to the amazement that a dream could seem so real that it took me several moments to realize that I was there in my own bedroom, what I had experienced was only a dream, not a nightmare by any stretch of the imagination, just a dream. It had seemed so vivid, so real.

My Father had come to me, beckoning that I should follow him. We walked across the open field to a depression that opened upon a room of good size.

There were boxes, bags and other storage units that appeared to be full and sealed. We opened the first box, which was filled with old children's books, dolls and various other memorabilia.

Then he led me outside through the basement door. Standing in the field was a large hot-air balloon, tethered and ready for takeoff. I climbed aboard as Daddy untied the restraining ropes and I was air-born.

Such magic appeared before my wonder filled eyes! The fields rolled on forever. There were no clouds in the sky, just dozens of other hot-air balloons drifting across the horizon in the light breeze. It was so beautiful, so serene.

Then I awoke with a start to the smell of coffee brewing in the kitchen. It was just a quiet dream.

* * * * * * * * *

LIVING TO LEARN AND LEARNING TO LIVE
Lea Meadow 3/9/13

When we come into this world, we are born naïve. Our eyes are still closed and our mind is empty (or so we shall believe, for who really knows what development has occurred within our brains?). Our mothers place us face up in our crib, which is our first outside residence upon surfacing from the security of the womb. This is done so that we shall not suffocate, which has a possibility if we are face down.

We then begin to explore what we can see with our limited scope of vision. We notice that our limbs, which appear attached to our torso, actually move. Our little arms flail around, up and down. We smile . . .but why? Is it a reflex of our developing nervous system, or an emptiness within our little belly looking for nourishment? Suddenly little feet appear in our line of vision, and we move them about as we did our arms. We are alive, our first lesson in living has been accomplished.

Our next lesson is more than likely the realization of our vocal cords. If we expel air, we probably can make noise through this opening in our face, which is our mouth. We are amazed at the rapid speed in which our mother comes to learn what discomfort had caused this outpouring of noise. She first explores the region of our anatomy where she has placed a soft large square of material. It seems to help confine the wet and smelly stuff we have placed there. After furnishing us with a clean cloth, she picks us up in her warm arms and carefully places us over her shoulder, tenderly patting our upper back, which prompts us to expel a rather loud noise, which is called a burp. Then she places us back in our comfortable bed, again face up, crooning a lullaby which soon puts us to sleep, which helps us restore the energy we used to accomplish all those deeds in living to learn has been accomplished. That was a relatively easy procedure. The next step is long, tedious, and frustrating.

    The lesson of "learning to live" has many steps and they never seem to end. It seems we are expected to manage many things in life by ourselves. We learn that if we "crawl" we can change our position. Mother places us on a small blanket on the floor. Outside the reach of our small bodies lie a number of interesting objects. To reach them, we must find a way to get to them, so we roll over on our stomachs and carefully hitch our way across the floor. The first object looks interesting. It is shaped so that our small fingers can grasp it. We pick the object up, which makes a noise we learn is a rattle. This is fun and we amuse ourselves until sleep overcomes us.

We crawl through life for a period of time until we decide this is really a slow way to explore. Somehow we are able to lift our rather pudgy body to a standing position and decide to move forward. Mistake number one, for we soon find we are back down on the floor. No one comes to our rescue, so we try again . . . and again, until success is ours. Look out world, here we come.

We will continue to fall down, get up and start all over again for as long as we are alive. Have we truly learned to life, or is living to learn a way of life? We persist and we endure.

* * * * * * * * *

A DAY IN THE FIELD OF LEARNING
Lea Meadow

Most of my story is found in my family biography, as I regress to my grandfather and his teaching experiences.

Last meeting of the Owen County Art Guild's

writers group, I had concentrated on "living and learning". As we heard, this is a lifetime experience, continuing on a daily basis.

Why do we pursue the paths we take in life? Some paths may be destined at the beckoning of others. My mother taught in a rural consolidated school in south western Minnesota. Her father was Superintendent of Schools in Jackson, Minnesota. Mother was the eldest daughter, and she may possibly have been influenced to be a member of the teaching community by her father. It did not please her that much, for this career lasted only one year.

However, she was very disappointed when I pursued the field of political science. I did, however, manage to accumulate a second major in English and enjoyed working on the school newspapers. Teaching was not in my vocabulary until much later in life, when I became a Title I reading teacher, inspiring third and fourth grade students that reading was fun.

The field of education opened another door for me, and I became a member of the Guidance

Office in a consolidated school district in western Massachusetts, which was a learning experience I will never forget. Follow my advice when I tell you, 'do NOT work in the same environment where your children pass your office every day on their way to class.' The urge to interfere on either part can be disastrous.

Mother had already left this earth when I worked in the field of education. I like to think that she smiled down at me from time to time, with what thoughts I can only imagine. In all truth and honesty, I would much prefer to write than to teach.

A good example of this aversion to teaching came when my daughter told her kindergarden teacher that she had learned to read in the bathroom. I shudder to think what magazine she was reading in the bathroom! She has turned out to lead a productive life, so she must have learned something in that little room!

* * * * * * * * *

I SAW A GLIMPSE OF HEAVEN
Lea Meadow 3/22/13

It was a cold afternoon in late December . . . the 27th to be exact. I had visited my OB-GYN doctor that morning. He told me to go take my mother and my husband to lunch, to go to the hospital after everyone had been fed and to wait for him to make his rounds.

One needs to understand that when my mother said "jump," you jumped. She had come to Long Island, New York, from her home in Sioux Falls, South Dakota, to help in the rearing of her first grandchild. Mother said I would have that baby that day, regardless of what the doctor said. Right on schedule, I awoke to find that my water had broken. A call to the Associated Press office in Manhattan to tell the expectant father the great news, his reply, "not now, there is a big breaking news story that tells of a prison riot in Attica, New York," and he was busy.

The prospect of fatherhood appeared to outweigh the prison outbreak, for he did head for home, my husband and my mother did have lunch, and we walked to the hospital where at approximately 4 pm a healthy, but bruised baby girl was born.

The bruises on that poor little girl were on her face. The tiny nose was as flat as one that belonged to a prize fighter. There was nothing wrong with her lungs, however. She could bellow out her needs for food and other of life's necessities. The problem seemed to be a result of acid indigestion. She was both bottle and breast fed.

This was just one of the glimpses I saw of heaven that beautiful day. The other was a different type of trauma. After giving birth, I was sent to the recovery room, where I was in no hurry to awaken.

When I finally opened my eyes, I knew that life had passed me by, for there I was in Heaven. The angels all wore blue and floated past my window in an eerie fashion, not speaking, but carrying on their heavenly duties.

I went back to sleep. When I awoke it was

evening. I had a roommate who was coughing persistently and no one in this fancy Fifth Avenue hospital seemed to care. I rang my bell, but no one came for what seemed an eternity.

Flower Fifth Avenue hospital was experiencing an all-out strike. The "angels" I had seen out the recovery room window were picketing nurses. Nurses in the hospital were scarcer than the proverbial "hen's teeth." I never "caught" pneumonia but did go home with laryngitis that lingered for a very long time.

That is how I saw a glimpse of heaven.

* * * * * * * * *

THE OLD CELLAR
Lea Meadow 3/29/13

It was a small house built in the early 1920's. The back entrance, the one we most often used, was at ground level. As you entered the door, directly in front of you was a root cellar, in which was stored such staples as potatoes and onions. To the right were three steps that led into the kitchen. On the left was the flight of stairs that descended into the cellar.

It was dark and dank down there and smelled like coal, which was the fuel used to stoke up the old furnace. As we moved from that cottage when I was only five years old, the possibility of my spending much time down there was more than likely very limited.

In order to have coal delivered to the house, the coal truck backed up to a window of the cellar, removed the glass from the window and proceeded to dump the coal down the chute.

When I was five, our family was increased by the addition of our little sister. Two small bedrooms were not large enough to hold the expanded family and we moved to a larger two story colonial across the driveway. The cottage was held as an income source and several couples later inhabited it.

The cellar, which became a second home to my sister and me, was in the new house. It consisted of two large rooms. To the right of the open stairs was the storage and laundry room, which always smelled like damp clothes. There were two or three wash tubs, one for washing the laundry, the second to rinse out the soap and wringing the clothes dry, so that you could hang them on the line, which was also in the cellar.

If you are old enough, you may remember the ordeal of rinsing the laundry . . . only after hand-scrubbing the clothes to get them clean. Then you wrung them out, and placed them in the rinse basin, where you used a plunger to expel the soap. No, there was absolutely nothing mechanical in these steps.

This is the cellar I remember best. The large room to the left of the stairs was the room in which Mother sewed all our clothes. At the far end were two twin beds, for those occasions when there were overnight guests. But, mostly, they were the place where we sisters spent long hours playing with our paper dolls.

These paper dolls were wonderful playmates. They were laboriously cut out from *Sears* and *Montgomery Ward's* catalogues. They had rooms full of furniture, also cut from those catalogues. A wonderful way to spend a rainy day. Those paper dolls took trips and did things we could only imagine.

There was a glitch in getting to that wonderful play area, however. The stairs were open in back, and imagination on my part, invented a family of bears who would reach up and grab young legs . . . especially those of little sister, who had a way of spoiling my imaginary escapades. Imagination is great until it affects the one who is using it wants to scare someone else. We quickly made it down those stairs.

I don't envy children of today, who spend hours in front of computers, or on ipods and cell phones texting their friends or playing mindless games of chance, such as *Free Cell* and *Solitaire*. There is no need to use one's imagination to accomplish these games. Have we eliminated the use of our brains to think, to imagine? How sad that would be.

* * * * * * * * *

AMAZING FACTS
Lea Meadow April 5, 2013

There are amazing facts to be found on any number of subjects. I have limited my search to the field of dreams, as I dream many dreams during the course of a night's sleep. Since I was diagnosed with the early stages of Alzheimer's, I have been taking a pill at bedtime, which the doctor told me has been known to cause the user to dream. Fortunately, they are gentle dreams, not nightmares.

Here are some facts, which I found while perusing the internet that are related to dreams:

Within five (5) minutes, you forget 90% of your dreams.

Blind people also dream, using senses of sound, smell, touch and emotion.

Everybody dreams.

An interesting fact, we only see faces we already know.

Not all dreams are in color.

Anxiety is the most common emotion in

dreams.

Negative dreams are more common than positive ones.

On the average, one has four (4) to seven (7) dreams per night. You will dream one or two hours every night.

Animals also dream.

REM, which means "rapid eye movement," is a normal stage of dreams. During REM the body is paralyzed and the physical body does not move.

These were some of the amazing facts that I learned while scrolling down the internet.

* * * * * * * * *

STRANGE NOISES IN THE DARK
Lea Meadow April 12, 2013

A terrible scream came from outside the bedroom window one early summer night when we lived in Arkansas. It was animal, not human, and seemed to be coming from the woods to the east of our property. Later we learned that a panther had caused the noise. One does not expect to hear a panther in a well-developed suburban area. Always the unexpected.

Strange noises in Indiana have given us cause to awaken in the middle of the night as well. One midnight we awoke to the howling of a coyote coming from the woods.

One night I awoke to a loud bang coming from outside the house. I was startled enough to arouse my mate to have him take a look (not timid me). He donned his trousers, grabbed a flashlight and proceeded outside. Nothing met his vision, so he went back to bed. In the morning we discovered a gust of wind had re-arranged the furniture on our enclosed deck and knocked down several wind chimes, causing this ruckus.

One early morning we awoke to find a herd of deer had found refuge outside our bedroom window. One might imagine that they were attracted to our many bird feeders and upon filling their bellies, decided to take a well-deserved nap before heading back to the woods. Deer make funny little squealing noises, their method of communicating with each other.

Not everyone or everything that visits in the night, however, makes any noise. We live between several ponds and on several occasions find that crawdads (or crawfish) have built little huts on the lawn. Once we saw the remains of one that had obviously found his demise from a passing cat, dog, or maybe even a fox or coyote, which also like to roam across our yard, which is the last yard in a well populated subdivision.

One never knows who or what all inhabit our yards while we are basking in the glory of sleep.

* * * * * * * * *

THE FAMILY FARM
Lea Meadow April 19, 2013

When gasoline rationing allowed us to travel, we journeyed the 90 miles east to visit Grandma and the various aunts, uncles and cousins on

Daddy's side of the family. Most of the Voss clan remained on the farm. Only Daddy, Uncle Ed, Uncle Jack and Aunt Viola ventured to life in the city, which left August, Hardy, Henry, Rudy and sister Bertha living on farms. Grandpa Voss had died long before I was born, but Grandma lived to be 94 before she died.

The two farms I remember best are the one owned by Uncle August, where many family reunions were held each September 1, on Grandma's birthday, and Uncle Rudy's large estate where we would meet for later family gatherings. Rudy's wife, my Aunt Hilda, was a large woman who had very ruddy cheeks and was an excellent cook. It was on Rudy's farm where I met up with a huge bumble bee and wound up with a sting between the ring finger and little finger on my right hand. The bee sting brought me under the diligent care of Aunt Viola, who administered layers of baking soda to draw out the stinger.

Uncle August had seven or nine children, a boisterous group of hungry farmers. He had two daughters who were loud, as well. My father detested farming and all that machinery. After my parents had been married for a year, they gratefully left the farm for city living in Sioux Falls, South Dakota. Daddy worked for two furniture stores in his lifetime of toil away from the farm. He sold and laid carpet and linoleum all over floors in Sioux Falls and the outlying counties until he retired at the ripe old age of 75.

However, the "farm" closer to home was planted in the vacant field next to our property in Sioux Falls at 1900 South Fourth Avenue. It was planted during the Second World War and sustained our family of five and the many Army soldiers stationed at the temporary air base in Sioux Falls who Daddy befriended and who visited our home. We raised many vegetables in that garden, so many that in order to raise the very necessary potatoes, we drove up to the end of Fourth Avenue (maybe a mile from home) where we planted long rows of potatoes. I was the designated "planter," following Daddy and his trusty hoe, sticking one small piece of potato, which always had an eye sticking up so the potatoes would develop, and carefully covered with top soil. All summer long Daddy and I would go up to the potato patch to weed and watch the progress of our planting endeavors.

Most memorable were the carrots. In order to preserve fresh carrots for the long winter and spring months to follow one needed a big metal barrel that was partially filled with sand and carrots were then carefully placed among the sand pebbles. A cover was placed over the barrel to keep the rodents from feasting on the long, back-breaking ordeal of planting and harvesting.

Everything we ate was not raised on the "farm." Between two garages was build a run for the many chickens we raised. Never will I forget the little baby chicks we got at Easter, which grew up with all the other fowl and were always distinguishable by the little colored pin feathers which were difficult to remove.

Our meat products were supplemented by the many, many pheasants Daddy religiously hunted every fall. We ate pheasant every which way except under glass. It was fried, baked, boned, eaten as a meat or found its way into stews, soups or the infamous Chow Mein. I don't recall ever eating it for breakfast, but noon and evening meals always seemed to have pheasant served one way or another, except on the nights when we ate chicken.

The family farm on Fourth Avenue in Sioux Falls is the one I remember best.

* * * * * * * * *

A TREE CLIMBING FOOL
Lea Meadow   April 26, 2013

Climbing trees has never been something I would venture to do, not even on a dare. In all truth and reality, if my feet never left terra firma, I would be more than content to stay firmly affixed to the ground, both feet well planted.

When living in Arkansas we had a small orchard with apple, cherry, plum and apricot trees.

We had any number of wild beasts that climbed these trees abundantly loaded with fresh fruit, to include a family of raccoons. It was a wonder to see these furry little fellows sitting high in an apple tree, presumably left by their mother. She didn't return and we were concerned about their health and well-being. We owned a General Store a few miles from our house and had one employee, Jill, who tended the store while we went to lunch or to the bank. Jill rescued animals left abandoned or injured, returning them to good health and back into the wilds. She came with a cage large enough to hold said raccoons and carefully returned them to the wilds.

Before moving to Arkansas we lived in rural Massachusetts, where we had twenty acres and raised poultry of all kinds. We had a 'summer' neighbor – a practicing psychologist who owned a cat. One day this cat decided to climb one of our trees where he promptly fell asleep. The neighbor came looking for his cat and when he found it high in the tree became quite flustered. He wondered what he would do to get the darned cat back on earth. He had no clue what to do.

We assured him that the cat would come down from the tree, if we would all just go away and leave him alone. Sure enough, once we left the cat was very happy to oblige.

No, I don't climb trees. I don't remember ever having done so. I sat in my sand pile, under a big apple tree in our back yard. If an apple fell at my feet, I surely ate it . . . or at least did so until I found they might have worms hiding under those pretty skins.

Eating the worms was okay, if they were in plain sight. But to unconsciously bite into one would have repelled me deeply.

* * * * * * * * *

A HAPPY HEART
Lea Meadow   May 3, 2013

It's a beautiful Spring morning, the sun is shining brightly through the east window, the birds are chirping merrily at the feeders in the backyard, and my heart is happy.

My spouse of 32 years is sitting in his comfy chair, sipping the first cup of coffee on this beautiful morning, all is right with the world.

We are awaiting the arrival of the children, all adults, to help us celebrate this anniversary of Mother's Day. I have just learned that this day of celebration was first celebrated in 1908 when Anna Jarvis held a memorial for her mother. By the 1920's Anna was disappointed with the commercialism of this day. Her holiday was adopted by other countries and is now celebrated all over the world. In 1912 Anna trademarked the second Sunday in May as Mother's Day. President Woodrow Wilson signed his name to the law passed by Congress establishing that Sunday as Mother's Day in the United States.

Thank you Anna Jarvis and Woodrow Wilson for honoring mothers all across America. My heart is happy for this beautiful day.

* * * * * * * * *

I ENTERED THE RACE
Lea Meadow   May 10, 2013

While living in a small community in western Massachusetts, I became interested in the town government of this small area. A friend suggested that I run for the position of Selectmen, on the Democratic ticket. Democrats were few and far between, the Republicans had ruled the roost for eons. It was time for a change.

Wow. I had more than one strike against me I) I was a Democrat; 2) I was a newcomer to the area; 3) I was a woman; 4) the man I ran against was the Road Superintendent and well-liked by all. The odds were not very favorable.

There were open house events to attend, people to meet, issues to address. There were a number of snide looks my way by the old-timers in town. So I campaigned, wrote numerous letters to constituents and newspapers, knocked on a few doors and WON.

    I stayed clear of the territory involving the Road Superintendent as I really knew little about country roads and their upkeep, enjoyed working with my constituents and fellow Selectmen, tolerated wives who didn't think I belonged in that prestigious crowd and survived two terms of office. Even went to a State convention in Boston and really had a good time.

    It was a different kind of race, far from my youth when I lived with lots of neighborhood boys and became their "pacer" for the practices they ran to compete in high school athletics.

    Now I "race" to keep up with daily living, and all these writing assignments drawn from a basket every Friday afternoon at the weekly meetings of the Owen County Art Guild Writer's group.

    * * * * * * * * *

THE SECRET INGREDIENT
Lea Meadow   May 17, 2013

The big day has finally arrived. Everyone congregates at the Owen County Art Guild for the infamous chef's delight. . . Belgian Waffles. Behind the apron and white cap is the happy, but busy, chef and his able assistant, ready to whip up the batter, warm up the waffle irons and try to satisfy the hungry mob gathering at the serving window.

The waffles disappear, basically faster than the griddles can turn them out. The assistant frantically attempts to carefully crack those eggs, making sure that no egg yolk mistakenly finds its way into the bowl of egg whites, which would be a drastic error. The assistant begins the gentle process of whipping up the egg whites, while the chef carefully adds the yolks to his batter.

Now comes the critical step of folding the egg whites into his batter. The waffle irons beep, heralding the moment of anticipated arrival. . . the irons are hot. The batter is carefully measured into the irons, the lids are closed and all wait with baited breath and growling tummies.

But wait. What is the secret ingredient? The freshness of the eggs, the proper temperature of the waffle irons? None of the above. It is the decision of which of the several toppings to pour over these works of art. Could it be strawberries, cool whip or maple syrup? Why not a dab of all three? You still have not learned his secret ingredient, nor shall you ever, for if you knew, it would no longer be a secret!

* * * * * * * * *

MY FAVORITE MEAL
AND WHERE I GO TO GET IT
Lea Meadow   May 24, 2013

Today is Sunday, the beginning of a new week. My favorite meal on Sunday is chicken, fixed however my favorite chef feels like doing it. We will probably have chicken breast served with mashed potatoes, broccoli and a salad. Sounds good to me!

Monday looms on the horizon. I discover the chef has relinquished the task of preparing the evening meal to me. Alas, we devoured everything that was fixed for yesterday ... no leftovers, so we start from scratch. Yes, Polish sausage and sauerkraut sound good to me. Now to sit quietly and read the book I started last night. Potatoes! Good, there are a couple left in the larder that can be mashed, or baked, to go with the meat and 'kraut.

Now it is Tuesday, and again, no leftovers from the day before. That's okay, we shall eat soup (canned) and cheese and crackers. A big bowl of ice cream around nine o'clock will satisfy the hungers before the final cup of tea before bedtime.

Wednesday means pasta. Neither one of us is an Italian, but we have had a tradition of pasta on Wednesdays for as long as I can remember, and a good supply is always on hand.

Thursday. Ugh. What to fix? Pork chops sound good to me. Yes, there are still some left in the freezer, which is beginning to look bare. Sounds like a trip to Bloomington and a stop at *Sam's* and *Kroger's* are becoming a reality.

Fridays are never a problem. Neither one of us is of the Catholic faith, but on Friday at our home it means fish. The choices are many, as we keep a good supply of fish on hand.

Saturday is pizza day. There's a pepperoni pizza in the freezer. Salad makings are in the 'frig, always ice cream in the freezer to top off the day.

Another week of menu planning has been successfully accomplished. The odds for a very similar array of goodies loom in the future for the week ahead. I can sit back; relax, while the chef does his thing. When it is time, he will call his able salad chef to fix the side bar and we shall dine in fashion.

* * * * * * * * *

DAD FELL HARD FOR MOM   June 1, 2013

My father truly loved his wife more than anyone or anything. Their beginning had been rough, in many ways. Mother loved to chide that "Lawrence this" or "Lawrence that", whenever she found a flaw in Daddy's armor. I remember him replying on many occasions that she should have settled for good ol' Lawrence.

When they were on their honeymoon on her Uncle Dick's ranch in North Dakota, there had been a hunting incident. Daddy had shot a rabbit, the bullet ricocheted off a rock and hit Mother in the left eye. A rush to the nearest hospital only soured the episode more, as the doctors could do nothing to save that eye. Mother wore a glass eye for the rest of her long (spoiled) life, for he certainly spoiled that dear lady. Mother could do no wrong.

Whether that adoration would have been so endearing if it had not been for that fateful accident, no one will ever know. Let it rest that she was a very pampered and adored bride for those many years.

* * * * * * * * *

ON A SUMMER EVENING
Lea Meadow June 7, 2013

It was a warm evening in June, time for our nightly walk before having a cup of tea and retiring for the night. The sky was overcast as we left the house, but rain did not seem to be in the immediate forecast, so we started our walk.

Going up the road north of our home, we traveled along in relative darkness. When we got to the top of the hill there was a clearing in the sky.

What to our wondering eyes did appear, a myriad of twinkling stars, more stars than the mind could absorb.

We continued along our walk, grateful to God for allowing the night to bring forth such splendor.

In the many walks we have taken since, none has equaled the brilliance of that one star-lit night.

* * * * * * * * *
THE WINNING NUMBER
Lea Meadow June 21, 2013

We were never a gambling couple, but one year for our anniversary my son gave us a ticket for the Massachusetts State Lottery. We went down the road to the local winery, which also dealt with the lottery and presented our ticket. We were surprised and delighted to discover we had won $169.

We were so certain that we were indeed destined to become rich from playing the lottery that we promptly purchased another ticket. That first win would become our last, and we stayed home and tended our large flock of various turkeys, geese, ducks and chickens.

Although gambling was not to be our game, until we left Massachusetts for Arkansas, we continued to "play the lottery." There is indeed, no fool like an old fool.

As so many of my short stories are, this, too is true.

* * * * * * * * * *

UPHILL
Lea Meadow   June 24, 2013

Whether we wish to admit it, every day we struggle uphill to make it through another twenty-four hour period. We struggle with the need to attend to our toilette, don the appropriate clothes and find some sustenance in the kitchen. First, I must have that necessary jolt of java, black, please. No cream and/or sugar for this gal!

After the second cup, I am ready to address the breakfast table. "Breakfast" is an Americanized version of "break the fast," or the first food of the new day. When the tummy has been satisfied, it is time to "meet the day" for sure. There are always the "chores" to be done . . . clear the table, rinse (at least) the dishes, make the bed, brush your teeth and prepare to tackle the day. You are on the bottom of the hill with a long haul ahead before the summit has been attained and bed once again calls you to your slumber.

As I sip that last bit of bedtime tea, I ponder

the question, did I achieve my goals for this day, or am I remiss in my expectations? Wow. What were my expectations, or did I have any set goals to attain?

I reminisce, 1) I did my exercises before getting up, I got dressed, had coffee, ate breakfast. 2) I surveyed the cupboards and refrigerator to discover I would need to go to the grocery in the morning, as lunch time foods were pretty much gone. 3) a stop at the library should be planned, as I finished the last book I had borrowed the previous week. Cannot be without a good book to read, if only at bedtime, a habit I have held for many, many years. Frankly, I would rather read some other bard's words than put down on paper my own thoughts. So off I go to town, shopping because eating is essential and to the library because next to eating, reading is very important to me.

To get to the library and the stores, I must travel UPHILL (there, I used the word) literally, as I live at the bottom of a hill and must travel several other hills before I reach the flatlands of the river area.

In the struggle to persist in living, we are faced with more up hills, than down hills. Our survival rests pretty much on our ability to face these many hills, day in and day out.

So, dear friends, upward and onward: another day has dawned.

* * * * * * * *

LET US HELP YOU
June 28, 2013

If you have ever been hospitalized or had physical therapy, the phrase "let us help you" is one with which you rapidly became acquainted: "here, let us help you with the bedpan," when all you want to do is get out of bed and use the nice little bathroom which your room has right there . . . not twenty feet from the bed. Even if you were able to make that maneuver, "they" have conveniently placed the forbidding rail in your way. Thus, out comes that ugly device known as the bedpan.

The day arrives when you are at last told it is time to take a walk. "Let us help you," chirp two husky nurses, one to lift you under the armpit on both sides, and "we" are ready to take that little walk. The emphasis is placed on the word "little." The door from your room to the narrow hallway is so close you can see every scrape and blemish, but that will seem to be the longest walk ever devised by man.

We are in the hallway. Doors to neighboring rooms are open and you espy others who are bedridden, looking longingly at you struggling to remain upright. You survive the extremely long days of suffering in the hospital. Your release is quickly thwarted when you learn that you have at least six weeks of physical therapy to endure. Understand, you only broke an arm, not a leg. You should be able to take care of yourself without someone standing beside you, prodding you on. It doesn't take long for you to realize that you need all the additional help that can be administered.

You cannot drive yourself to these therapy sessions, so the spouse helps you tenderly get situated in the automobile and carefully (and so it seems, very slowly) wend the way down the road. It would have been nice if the facility was located closer to home, but you grudgingly sit beside the driver, trying not to feel all the bumps and hollows that seem to have appeared on the road ahead.

At last you arrive at your destination. What's this? Why do they insist that you must sit in a wheelchair just to go from the car to the front door, and then sit in that chair until you're finally wheeled into the therapy room, where two very able bodied nurses are on hand to lead you through a regimen of exercised designed to make you get better. Actually it feels kind of nice to have someone gently massage all those aches and pains. You even feel almost human for the next three or four days, and then you long for the next session.

There are a number of incidents in your life where someone comes up to you and says, "let me help you"; the eager sales clerk in the department store who is sure such and such item will look just great and loads your arms with several garments, which you take into the little dressing room for a fitting. After several feeble attempts to find just the right item, not to mention the proper fit, I could swear I wear a size 16, but I guess all those "made in China" wearing apparel are sized differently from the ones you used to be able to afford that said "made in the USA".

To me, the most dreaded experience of this "let me help you" is when the nice Boy Scout insists upon helping you across the street.

* * * * * * * * *

MISSING YOU
Lea Meadow July 5, 2013

Mother has been gone since 1978, but there are times when I still miss her. Oh, she could be a terror, always there when you wished she was somewhere else, and not around when you needed her most.

She had an uncanny knack for saying the wrong thing, such as the time I fell and scraped my knee something fierce. She could apply a bandage to the banged up knee while wondering aloud what I had done to the poor sidewalk. Certainly made you quit bawling and start wondering why the sidewalk was more important than your knee, which hurt something awful.

Then there were times when she did something that would make you both laugh so hard you were crying beyond belief, like the time she had a few too many and fell backwards into the bathtub while trying to negotiate the doorway. We laughed and laughed when I grabbed her hands and pulled her out.

Mother had been a teacher before she married Dad. It was a small country one-room schoolhouse, but she ruled the roost. She spent many hours with me when I was very young, teaching me the art of listening while she read from *The Children's Book of Knowledge*, the many volumes we had. The first book held many, many verses of poetry and simple stories such as *Jack and the Beanstalk, Rumplestiltskin* and many, many others. I would sit on her lap for as long as she could tolerate reading.

When I was older and able to read myself, we would spend hours after supper taking turns reading to each other. I gave those books to my daughter and they still sit on a bookshelf in the guest bedroom of her home.

Of course there were those times when I grew older that she would be sitting in the living room when I came stumbling in way past a proper bedtime for a high school lass. Those were memorable times, but pleasant.

I wore a leather flight jacket, which was the "in thing" of the time. Her nose was very keen, for she could smell the cigarette residue on that jacket and could tell by the look in my eyes that I had not just been riding around with the girls.

I have a saying that I did in cross stitch which reads, "Mirror, mirror on the wall, I'm just like Mother after all." Not because I remember too many times (my sons would argue that one) sitting waiting for the boys to come home.

I never had that need with their older sister as she went away to "early college" when she was sixteen. What time she might have come home to the dorm, I have no clue. She is my daughter, and I would therefore assume much like her mother in many respects.

Yes, Mother, I miss you still, especially when I have read a good book, seen a good play or had an outstanding meal. I don't miss those times when you reprimanded me . . . oh, there was the time when I did something that upset you and you sent me to my room without supper. But, Daddy saved the day when he came into the bedroom with a dish of ice cream.

Did you know that?

* * * * * * * * *

LOOKING FOR A HOME
Lea Meadow July 12, 2013

How does one go about looking for a home? I can only attest to how we have accomplished this feat. My first home was chosen by my parents who were living in a cute little bungalow in Sioux Falls, South Dakota, with two small bedrooms. I shared one of those bedrooms with my sister, who was eleven years old when I was born. When the family increased with the addition of my little sister (younger by five years) we moved across the driveway to the bigger Colonial style house, where the family thrived for many years.

The folks remained in that big house until after all the girls left home. Then they moved back across the driveway to the bungalow, where they remained for the rest of their lives.

When I moved to eastern New York State, we first lived in an apartment. After the first child was born, we bought a nice little Cape Cod style home further out on Long Island, where we remained until we moved to Egremeont, Massachusetts. My husband was working for the Associated Press and had been transferred to the Albany, New York bureau. I answered an ad in a newspaper, and we settled in an old converted carriage house, where we remained for a number of years, raising our three children. When the big house across the street from the carriage house became available, we moved across the road to the big house. I was divorced when I met my present husband, who had five children. So now we filled the rooms with eight children, a dog and numerous cats. In the back yard we established a small poultry farm, utilizing several small buildings which we moved there to house our chickens, adding additional buildings for ducks, geese and turkeys. These critters not only furnished us with all the poultry we could eat, but enough to sell dressed birds for adoring clients, which helped pay for the feed.

    When the eight children grew up and moved on to their own dreams, we put our fingers on a map, and moved to northeastern Arkansas, where we operated a general store for five years before retiring. We had no home at the time and lived in a small room at the back of the building that would become the *TLC General Store.* When the store was ready to open we bought 20 acres in the country north of the little town of Williford. The store consisted of two rooms. One became the grocery store, complete with a deli where we made sandwiches for people who stopped by to see what was happening. We also sold ice cream cones and made super sundaes. The second room became my yarn shop. When we had lived in Massachusetts I had a yarn shop in one of the front rooms on the main floor. So we not only sold eggs and poultry, but yarn and fabrics. The yarn shop goods traveled with us to Indiana. I have much embroidery floss left today, and sadly it is stored in the original bins in the garbage; sadly, because I hardly ever use any of it. My sewing endeavors have taken a far back seat since moving to Indiana.

    When we closed the store after five years, we lived in that small house until we built a much larger one, a very much larger one, which I designed. There were a total of thirteen rooms in that house, no basement, but an upstairs balcony that consisted of two large bedrooms separated by a large bathroom.

One day we decided to move back up North to be nearer to South Dakota, where my sister lives, and equally as far a distance to Massachusetts, where my youngest son lives. I also have a daughter living in Nashville, Tennessee and a son in Clarksville, Tennessee.

Putting a finger on the map, we ended up in an apartment in Spencer, Indiana. We very shortly found a piece of property west of town, built our present home, which is one third the size of the one in Arkansas, where hopefully we will spend the rest of our lives. That's how we found our homes.

* * * * * * * * *

MORE ON LOVE
Lea Meadow July 19, 2013

We first experience love when we entered this world, the love of a mother and a father. We are cuddled and coddled, cared for with all the tenderness two adoring adults can give. It is warm.

We attain the age when we are ready to leave the confines of this home to attend school. We enter kindergarten, where we find a caring and loving teacher who will guide us to the experience of developing friendships outside the family. These early teachers are loving and kind, helping us learn the skills which will establish the foundation of our beginning of a new kind of learning.

We will spend the nest thirteen years attending school. When you successfully finish one grade, you are promoted to the next level of learning. When I was a youngster, we went to elementary school from kindergarten through eighth grade, when we graduated to go on to higher education at High School, which included grades nine through twelve.

During the High School years we more than likely experienced what we thought was love for a person of the opposite sex. This could be a one-way experience, if your heart was set on some fellow who didn't see you for more than someone who might let him look at your theme paper, or a quick glance across the aisle to the answers on your test paper. Even that slightest of interest would send your heart pitter-pattering, until you found him walking closely to some other girl, as they wended their way to the next class. Heart break number one, with the forecast looking full of such disappointments.

Eventually you find a soul mate, a person of the opposite sex who has the look of caring in his eyes. It may mean nothing to him, but your heart is set on winning him over to your way of thinking. If you are lucky enough to find Mister Right, it is quite advisable to hang on, NOT to cling so tightly as to scare him off, but firmly enough to help him like you enough that love will blossom. Yes, indeed, love is warm.

* * * * * * * * *

THE LIGHT THAT TWINKLED
Lea Meadow   July 26, 2013

There are many lights that twinkle; most of them are stars in the sky. If you are fortunate to live in the country and you enjoy a stroll down the lane after dark, your eyes will behold many twinkling lights in the heavens above.

One evening we started out stroll. The skies were overcast, the road ahead dim to see. Suddenly, as we reached the top of a hill, the heavens opened up to a vista beyond belief, trillions of sparkling, twinkling stars led our way. It was a sight to behold, and one that we have rarely seen since.

One evening my daughter was upstairs and supper was ready to serve. My husband went to the landing and called up to her. She put on the light to descend the narrow back stairs and the light went out. She diligently flipped it back on, and off it went again. The game continued for a few minutes, she would flip it on; George would turn it off, so on and off it went, until he tired of playing the game.

I have done the same as a child, toying with my younger sister. Telling her that bears lived under the stairs was bad, but constantly leaving her behind on the dark basement stairs was worse.

Artificial lights blinking and twinkling are one thing. When Mother Nature shows her abilities, it is a talent worthy of watching. "Twinkle, twinkle, little star," I truly wonder what you are.

* * * * * * * * *

A MOTHER'S LOVE
Lea Meadow August 9, 2013

When you glimpse at a picture of the Madonna holding the baby Jesus, you are drawn to the look of admiration, adoration and love shining on her face. Such is the love of a mother to her offspring; those moments of joy when she holds the infant in her arms for the first time. She is overwhelmed by a sense of pride and awe that this perfect little specimen spent its first months snuggly secure within her womb is already becoming an individual who will consume many hours of her time, and cause many hours of anxiety as he or she becomes a person in their own right.

A mother finds great pleasure in seeing the child take its first wobbly step toward independence. She is concerned for the safety of the child as he or she takes this great leap to independence and she is never truly ready to lose any of her control; letting go is never easy.

A mother sends her child off to the care of others; teachers, ministers, friends, who will help in the development of her precious child to assure that they are taught not only the good things life will bring, but also the pitfalls that will be there along the way. She must learn to accept that others will spend a great deal of time and energy in the development of her child's character. As the school bus pulls away from the curb, the mother has lost a great deal of control over that development, but must be there to render the encouragement that only she can give, realizing some control has been delegated to others.

When the child leaves the confines of high school and elects to travel down the road of higher education, a mother frets that others will influence the child in ways unacceptable to her beliefs. The mother worries about the child's interest in members of the opposite sex and wonders if she has done all that is possible to install the proper values. Will the child find a mate who will cherish her offspring in an acceptable manner? Will she find that as she becomes a grandmother she should remain in the background as a guiding influence, not as a busybody telling someone else how to raise this new child?

The child reaches adulthood and feels confident that it can find the way without the guidance of mother. It doesn't take long to realize what comfort exists in the knowledge that mother is at worst a phone call away from guidance.

The father may remain the primary enforcer of discipline, but the mother will be the guiding influence of the behavior, as she is the "home maker," the one who is more often spending the majority of the time in the upbringing of the children.

A mother's love is multi-encompassing. She must be firm but understanding to the many complexities that greet the child as it moves down the road to independence. She must learn to love and let go.

A mother's love is forever-enduring.

* * * * * * * * *

I LOVE BOOKS
Lea Meadow August 16. 2013

I am forced to leave the comfort of my favorite chair, put down a very exciting historical novel to write why "I Love Books". That could be enough said, but I shall continue.

As a small child, my mother read to me endlessly from the *Children's Garden of Verse*, which was an eight volume set of stories designed for the different age groups. When I became old enough to read for myself, it was time for me to read to my little sister, five years my junior. We were back to nursery rhymes, good old standards like, *"Jack be Nimble," "Hickory, Dickory, Dock,"* graduating to stories such as *"Goldilocks and the Three Bears,"* and *"Rumplestiltskin."*

Although my daughter never had any children of her own, that set of books still resides in her bookcase in the guest bedroom. It would be nice if when her nieces and grandnieces came to visit that they would open the covers to these books and be enthralled with the fairy tales of my youth.

I love to read. Today I go to the local library and bring home four or five books of my choosing. I sold most of my books to the new owner of the house in Williford, Arkansas, as I had read them all. They are heavy and would have added a great deal of additional cost to a move to Indiana, storage space to keep them all while our house was built, etc. In the past I was a member of the *Literary Guild* and the *Book of the Month Club*.

The *Owen County Public Library* in Spencer has a wonderful array of books for me to check out. I am a very frequent visitor to that establishment, where I tend to gravitate to the mysteries and historical novels.

Now that I have enlightened you with my tale of loving books, please excuse me while I retire to my favorite recliner and read some more.

* * * * * * * * *

A CALL FROM THE WILD
Lea Meadow September 6, 2013

We live in a well-developed community where a stretch of state highway ran. We were accustomed to noises from animals, especially cattle, dogs and cats. Once a family of raccoon climbed our apple tree and lost all reasoning as how to descend. A friend of ours saved wild animals from injury and death. She came over and carefully extracted the coons from the tree. They promptly made a hasty retreat.

One day, a horrible scream came across our land, not human or anything we had ever heard before. The next day we read the local newspaper that a large black panther had been seen roaming the area. Where he came from, or even where he went, we never learned.

If you live in the country or in a small rural community, the possibility of hearing strange noises will probably greet you one day. When we lived in Arkansas we had the privilege of watching a wolf prance across our back yard. We had a small chicken coop in the back yard, and went to investigate the buildings for signs that he had found the door open to the hen house. It didn't appear that any of our fowl was missing, and we never saw the wolf again. On several occasions we also saw a fox circling the hen house, and there was always the threat of coyotes that we could see from the house. We had several deer sleep up near the house, presumably to feel secure from predators that roam the area.

We live in the last house in a subdivision here in Indiana. Just this morning we watched a gaggle of Canadian geese amble across our yard, munching on grass, stretching their wings and enjoying the morning sunrays. Suddenly, with no apparent warning, they took to the air and flew south.

We enjoy feeding the wild birds and watching them in our back yard. It is nice to have other creatures from the wild visit and not have them feel threatened. We are glad that we live in such an environment.

* * * * * * * * *

THE BARN WAS HAUNTED
Lea Meadow September 13, 2013

We lived in a well-developed rural area. We were accustomed to noises from animals, especially cattle, dogs and cats. But nothing had prepared us for unusual, spooky noises coming from the big barn at the end of the driveway where we lived in an old converted carriage house.

When we moved to the country, we were real city slickers, never having lived on a farm, so this would be an adventure. My husband was employed in a city about 60 miles from our new home. He would only be home on weekends, and had no desire to be a gentleman farmer.

On the other hand, I thought it would be the ideal place to raise three young children, and got right into the habits of country living. We soon had a goat, several sheep, a pony and two horses. It was time to load up the hayloft in the old barn and start feeding the beasts.

We had a dog and a cat. They both liked to visit the old barn where mice and other creatures lived. When we put hay in the loft, the cat was right there to make sure everything was in the proper place. He would climb up into the hayloft and sleep for hours.

But suddenly the cat refused to go into the barn. I kept hearing strange noises coming from the general direction of the barn, but attributed it to sounds of children playing and did not investigate further. In the spring I planted a large garden. In the fall it was time to harvest the crops and find a place to store all the food. So I purchased a freezer and placed it in a small area near the front of the barn where the stalls still existed from when the farmer had a number of cattle.

It was a strange setting, as the barn had a number of smaller rooms where the cows each had a stall, and the farmer milked the cows. As we did not have cows, the barn became a hide-away for my children. We had an old piano in the barn. Occasionally I would hear music coming from the piano, and assumed the children were playing the piano. But I often heard the piano being played when the children were all in the house.

One day I became brave and ventured out to the barn to see who was playing the old piano. No one was there and the piano was not playing by itself. I shrugged my shoulders and headed back to the house. About half way to the house I heard music coming from the barn. How could that be?

No one had been anywhere near the barn when I was just there.

I don't believe in ghosts and things that go bump in the night, but I must confess that going to the barn was something that I avoided as much as possible. I truly believe that old barn was haunted. I don't know whose ghost was there or why, so I will just chalk it up to one of those mysterious things that happen now and then.

* * * * * * * * *

ADVENTURES OF MY LIFE
Lea Meadow September 20, 2013

My life has been full of adventures. My dictionary tells me that an adventure is: "1) an undertaking of a hazardous nature, a risky enterprise, 2) an unusual experience or course of events marked by excitement and suspense; 3) participation in hazardous or exciting experiences."

We will stop there and begin to analyze some of my adventures. Many of them are relics from the decade when I served in one capacity or another doing "town business". I was elected to a three-year stint as a "Selectman" which is the equivalent to an Indiana alderman or councilman. The little town where I resided was basically of the Republican mantra. I came from a background of South Dakota Republicans and horrified my mother when I registered to vote as a Democrat. That tradition I carried with me when my husband and I moved to Massachusetts. Fortunately for me, my neighbor was proud to be a Democrat and urged me to run for office of Selectman. It was a close election, but I squeaked by my opponent with a slim six count lead (I don't remember, but feel quite confident that a recount occurred).

It is always an emotional journey when you relive the past, but I am tough and survived the hours we spent going through the box of the past.

This perusal of old stuff has led us to wonder what is in some of the other boxes left packed since we left Arkansas. Some of them are marked "save for a rainy day" and although we have more than likely had many rainy days in the past number of years, the boxes are still sitting there, waiting for us to have another adventure.

* * * * * * * * *

ABOUT THE AUTHOR

NANCY THURSTON
aka Lea Meadow

Born June 27, 1934, Sioux Falls, South Dakota

"I was the middle child of three daughters born to Ernest and Betty Voss. There were eleven years in age difference between my oldest sister and me and five between me and my younger sister."

"We lived in two houses while growing up. My sister, Virginia and I were raised in a small two bedroom bungalow at 1800 South Fourth Avenue."

"When Peggy arrived in 1939, it was time to move to larger digs. So, a two story Colonial was built right across the driveway at 1830 South Fourth Avenue, the little house was rented out and when the war came along, the big house was not only filled with siblings, but many dates for Virginia."

"Sioux Falls was home to an Army Air Base.

Our parents were both active in Sertoma, an organization that thrives today. The long name is 'Service to Man'."

"Virginia (always called Jimmy because she was supposed to be a boy) and mother were active in the USO. Our house resembled a small hotel on weekends when soldiers escaped the base to enjoy home cooking and go pheasant hunting with Ernie."

"Pheasant was a staple at our house: baked, fried, stewed, chow mien and soup. Don't think we ever had it for breakfast, but maybe."

"Our property was located at the dividing line for two elementary schools. Kindergarten found me enrolled in Mark Twain, but by third grade the lines had moved and Longfellow became home through the eighth grade. Then we transferred to the only high school, Washington, located downtown. I had nightmares for many years where I was late to class and had to climb multiple flights of stairs between classes."

"I began my literary career in High School, not as a journalist, but as the Advertising

Manager! I did take journalism classes, edited the local school newspaper and had several short articles included in the school magazine."

"I have participated in several plays. I was the Princess in fourth grade. The one who ate the pea, cried a lot and had one line: 'pass me another handkerchief, please'. Jimmy was a college student by then and her drama class put on the play 'Watch on the Rhine'. Two children actors were required and I was the little girl."

"We children got measles, which we promptly transmitted to the college students. Much pancake makeup was applied to all cast members. Also, sister Jimmy crashed through a glass door upon entering the stage, bled lots . . . but the play went on! Such drama!"

"Since then I have concentrated on writing. Not a steady diet, and certainly nothing that has benefited me with an income, but an enjoyable hobby."

"Before the age of the computer, everything was written in long hand, in spiral bound notebooks. Yes, I still have them all!"

"Jimmy, the journalist, kept diaries . . . many, many diaries. You will never learn anything personal about her from those diaries, just where they went. The most boring books I have ever read."

"Even today I keep a journal of sorts. They used to be quite explicit, loaded with feelings (and I had lots). Today they are pretty dull, just what we did today, where we went . . . don't stay home much!"

"Some time ago, I decided that if I was to be a serious writer, I needed a *nom de plume*, thus "Lea Meadow" was born. There is a duplicity there, if you hadn't noticed, as 'lea' and 'meadow' mean the same thing. The 'meadow' is a derivative of the Dutch name, 'Middaugh', which was my mother's maiden name."

"Many pages in my family history regard the Middaugh family, their lives in Holland and the migration to America. One day I will become serious and get that history in book form. It sits here in my computer, waiting for me to finish reading what others write, and join the ranks."

"To learn more about Lea Meadow, aka Nancy Jane Voss Lehmbeck Thurston, you must wait for The Book. Life is getting shorter and I have miles to go before I sleep."

* * * * * * * * *

EDITOR'S NOTE

Nancy is a highly educated woman with a vast and varied background of work and personal experience.

She has been a Certified Firefighter, choir member, Selectman, Town Treasurer, Member of the Executive Board of Campfire Girls, Massachusetts State PTA secretary, Finance Committee member and church moderator. She is a member of the National League of American Pen Women and of the Daughters of the American

Revolution.

    Her writing is as fascinating as her life. She can make the reader laugh or weep with equal expertise. Her travels and interest in genealogy add richness to her writing. Her vivid imagination serves well as she clearly conveys her message as she writes, be it history, fiction, humor or seriousness with apparent ease.